"UNDERSTANDING" THE ONENESS OF GOD

AND THE CONSPIRACY AGAINST JESUS CHRIST AND THE CHRISTIAN CHURCH

WILL DANIELS

WESTBOW
PRESS
A DIVISION OF THOMAS NELSON
& ZONDERVAN

Scripture taken from the King James Version of the Bible unless otherwise indicated.

WestBow Press books may be ordered through booksellers or by contacting:

WestBow Press
A Division of Thomas Nelson & Zondervan
1663 Liberty Drive
Bloomington, IN 47403
www.westbowpress.com
1 (866) 928-1240

ISBN: 978-1-4908-3036-0 (sc)
ISBN: 978-1-4908-3038-4 (hc)
ISBN: 978-1-4908-3037-7 (e)

Library of Congress Control Number: 2014904850

Printed in the United States of America.

WestBow Press rev. date: 3/31/2014

FOR THE LOVE OF
JESUS CHRIST
(YESHUA HAMASHIACH)

All glory and honor goes to our Lord and Saviour Jesus Christ (Yeshua HaMashiach), of whom, this book is dedicated. Over the years, the Lord has given us an insight into his love for humanity through the power of his Holy Word.

What you have in your hands is a miracle God has given to the world in these last days. God wants his people to return to the "Shema". God's oneness is the rock and foundation of our Christian journey and we must return to the Apostles' Doctrine and the oneness of God through his Son Jesus Christ (Yeshua HaMashiach) (Deuteronomy 6:4, Revelation 1:7-8).

Jesus Christ has been a steady rock in my life of ups and downs. Every thought, every word, every scripture comes from the revelations God has whispered in my ear over the years. As a man, I could do nothing; God gets all the glory, praise, and honor for all of his goodness and his understanding of the weaknesses of men.

Without the help of the Spirit of Christ, there is no way I could have understood all of the mysteries and nuances God has shown me. In the process of writing both books, "Understanding" the Trinity, and "Understanding" the Oneness of God," God would give me a thought early in the morning, and then He would give me an understanding of how to structure the concept concerning His Deity. I might lie in bed for hours just trying to understand what God was showing me and how the thought would be laid out in the book. Once I get up and start to write, God would show me scriptures I have read before but I never understood the connection to what God was showing me about His "Oneness".

At times, I would write for days just sleeping, eating, and writing. When you see all of the scriptures used, you would have to understand God showed every one of them to me and showed me how scripture fit with the concepts He was showing me. I didn't have a clue where most of these scriptures were.

On occasion, God would put a book in my path which addressed the exact subject he had shown me through meditation. For example, God used Sue Collins to give me a book by Muncia L. Walls called, *"That I May Know Him,"* which was instrumental in giving me another insight on understanding the oneness of God. God gets all the glory for what He has done and how he uses us to help prepare the world for his coming.

Focus

Repetition = Memorization

CONTENTS

FOREWORD

"And without controversy great is the mystery of Godliness: God was manifest in the flesh, justified in the Spirit, seen of angels, preached unto the Gentiles, believed on in the world, received up into glory" (I Timothy 3:16).

Blake Pascal said, "There is a God shaped vacuum in the heart of every man which cannot be filled by any created thing, but only by God, the Creator, made known through Jesus".

For centuries, that vacuum has propelled man's quest to know God. God declares in Isaiah 55:9 that "For as the heavens are higher than the earth, so are my ways higher than your ways, and my thoughts than your thoughts". Yet the invitation of Jesus is to "learn of me". (Matthew 11:29). Indeed, in his discourse on Mars' hill to the men of Athens, Paul asserted God is "... not far from every one of us" (Acts 17:27).

Each individual's concept of God determines and defines his relationship with Him. It is imperative that a believer prayerfully search the scriptures and mine the nuggets of truth contained therein concerning the question of who God is.

I have been privileged to observe Will Daniels' hunger and passion to know God more perfectly. He is an ardent advocate for and defender of truth and has faithfully followed Peter's admonition to "...grow in the grace and knowledge of our Lord and Saviour Jesus Christ". (II Peter 3:18). I urge the reader to carefully consider the discussion of God's identity that is contained in the pages of this book.

R.P. Kloepper II, M.D.

Acknowledgements

I would like to thank Michael Williams, Pastor of The Pentecostals of Apopka, Apopka, Fla., (Sermon: "The Fearful"). I can't tell you how many personal and spiritual challenges I have experienced while writing these books. When I really needed a Word from the Lord, God would speak to me through the anointed voice of Pastor Williams. Pastor Williams' dynamic and electrifying sermons will take you to a higher understanding of what God has in store for your life.

I would like to thank Dr. Ray Kloepper II MD., (The Forward), whom God has used on many occasions, and who has taken an interest in my writings and has offered suggestions and proofreading. The preaching of Dr. Kloepper helps us understand, through his experiences, our own personal relationship with Jesus Christ.

I would like to thank Bishop Billy G. Newton, Pastor of the Word of God Church, Diocesan of the 29th Episcopal District of the Pentecostal Assemblies of the World, Inc. Orlando, Fla. Bishop Newton coined the term, "bewilderment of the Trinitarian Doctrine," which is used to explain how we have strayed from the absolute oneness of God.

I would like to thank Bishop David K. Bernard, General Superintendent, United Pentecostal Church International, who is one of the greatest oneness writers of our times. He is a prolific writer who has written volumes on the "Shema" and the Deity of Jesus Christ.

I would like to thank Rabbi Ralph Messer, President and Founder of Simchat Torah Beit Midrash (STBM) and the International Center for Torah Studies, (ICTS) (torah.tv) for allowing me to use excerpts from his book, TORAH: LAW OR GRACE? Kingdom PRINCIPLES for Kingdom LIVING. Rabbi Messer is a master teacher on the foundational relationship between the Law (Torah – God's teaching and instruction), the Tanakh, and the New Testament.

I would also like to give thanks to my family and my lovely wife Dorothy who has been with me for over 45 years. God could not have given me anyone or anything better than what I have in my wife Dorothy. I also dedicate this book to our three children and five grandchildren.

PREFACE

Throughout this book, we will use the Hebrew name for Jesus which is Yeshua-meaning "Jesus is salvation". The Greek name Yesous/Iesous is translated into Latin Iesus and finally Iesus was translated into English as Jesus.

Theologians in an effort to understand the Deity of Jesus Christ, salvation, and the power of God's name, have used Hebrew, Greek, Latin, and English names for Jesus, never collectively settling on one name.

The following names; Yahoshua/Yahshua/Yehoshua/Yeshua, Y'shua, Iesous, Yesous, Iesus, and Jesus are examples of this type of disagreement. Scholars don't agree on what language to use, what name to use, and how or when to use God's name for salvation. Let's take a look at the meaning of the names.

1. Yahoshua/Yahshua–Hebrew-Messiah=Jesus Christ (Yahshua) is salvation.
2. Yeshua–Hebrew-Messiah=Jesus Christ (Yeshua) is salvation (used by Messianic Jews).
3. Y'shua–Hebrew–Messiah=Jesus Christ (Y'shua) is salvation (short for Yeshua).
4. Iesous-Greek–Messiah=Jesus Christ (Iesous) is salvation.
5. Yesous-Greek-Messiah=Jesus Christ (Yesous) is salvation.
6. Iesus-Latin–Messiah=Jesus Christ (Iesus) is salvation.
7. Jesus–from Greek, Latin to English=Jesus is the Messiah and salvation.

Dr. Neil Snyder, University of Virginia Professor (retired) wrote a book called, "His name is Yahweh" to prove Jesus is Yahweh and Yahweh is our Saviour, using, Isaiah 45:21-24, Philippians 2:9-11, John 8:58, 17:6, 11-12, 26 and Isaiah 43:11, as some of his foundational scriptures. In other words, Yeshua is Yahweh, meaning Jesus is God (Lord).

Most scholars are referring to the same Person, just a different name and a different understanding of that name, In addition, they can't agree on how His name is used in the "born again" experience (Acts 4:12).

Jesus Christ names can be used interchangeably, specifically, Yehoshua and Yeshua. I chose to use the name Yeshua in this book because of its foundation in the Hebrew Scriptures and to validate the name used by Messianic Jews. In other words, Jesus Christ in Hebrew is Yeshua HaMashiach.

Thus you will find the names, Jesus Christ and Yeshua, used in the book for clarification of the relationship between English and Hebrew and to prove Jesus Christ is Lord (Yeshua HaMashiach is Yahweh). We will show by scripture that we are talking about the same Person who is the God of Abraham, Isaiah, Jacob (John 10:30, 33).

If you would visit a Messianic Jewish Congregation you will find they use the Hebrew name Yeshua (Jesus) or they will use Yeshua HaMashiach (Jesus Christ). Occasionally, Messianic Jews will use the name Jesus when they are reading the New Testament. Now, the question is this; what name do we use for God since we don't want to be disrespectful to God by using the wrong name?

People from around the world have a different translation for the highest name of God yet, we, who speak English might not recognize it. God looks on the heart of a man, therefore, God recognizes the highest name you would use for Him based on your culture and your language.

Our language and culture is based on the English name Jesus Christ, therefore, our highest and most sacred name for God is Jesus Christ. God recognizes his highest name in any language and in any form; therefore, Jesus Christ is not a violation of the Word of God. Let your heart speak for you and use that name for God. God is a highly intelligent being and he knows you and your language and He recognizes your highest name for Him.

In addition to God recognizing His name in any language, we have found throughout the Old and New Testaments and the pages of this book; God is absolutely one Person. According to Colossians 2:9, we find through research Yeshua is Yahweh and Yahweh is Jesus Christ, same Person. God was revealed in one Person and three manifestations; the Father, the Son, and the Holy Ghost. (Genesis 17:1, Revelation 1:7-8, Deuteronomy 6:4, Luke 2:11, Isaiah 7:14, 9:6, Matthew 28:19)

God is absolutely one God and one Person
and it can be proven Biblically.

In these last days, God is bringing all faiths and religions into the knowledge of himself and the "oneness" of His nature through the mystery and knowledge of the gospel of Jesus Christ. Over the years we have lost our focus about the oneness of God and the Deity of Jesus Christ. And we must understand when and where the greatest conspiracy against Jesus Christ and the Christian Church started.

In Christendom there are 3 major concepts of Christianity that came out of the Nicene Council 325AD and the Council at Constantinople 381AD. Having three (3) difference groups or types of Christianity is a trick of the enemy. These Christian theologies can't agree on who God is. They can't agree on whether God is one God, two gods/persons, (one subordinate to the other) or three co-equal, co-eternal gods/persons. But I have some good news!! After reading this book, you will never be confused again about who God is and the oneness of His nature.

At the end of each chapter, you will find the following caption with scriptures, which will be a culmination of understanding the oneness of God in the Old and New Testaments. This is the caption;

"Jesus is Lord (Yeshua is Yahweh)"
(Gen. 17:1, Deut. 6:4, Isa. 9:6, 43:11, Luke 2:11,
John 1:10, 8:24, 58, Titus 2:13, Rev. 1:7-8)

The purpose of this caption is to help you remember "Jesus is Lord" and you will also remember the scriptures associated with the statement after you have finished reading the book. I want you to understand the oneness of God, who He is, salvation, and the power of God's name (Acts 4:12).

Don't try to remember the scriptures. Just read the caption "Jesus is Lord" (Yeshua is Yahweh) at the end of each chapter and read the scriptures. Close your eyes and see if you see the caption and the scriptures in your mind's eye.

If you can't see or remember the scriptures, don't be alarmed and don't try to remember them. Go to the next chapter; read the chapter, then, read the caption and scriptures. Close your eyes again and see if you can see the caption and the scriptures. Do this after reading each chapter throughout the book.

At the end of the book, you will not only understand "Jesus Christ is Lord" and the one God of heaven and earth, you will also understand how the following concepts and analogies can be understood. You will understand how the oneness of God can be presented to family and friends using the scriptures you have remembered.

We won't ever understand the Trinity but we can understand the oneness of God. For example; you should remember the following natural analogies which will be explained and relate them to your spiritual understanding of the oneness of God. You should remember;

1. The properties of water
2. Jumping out of an airplane without a parachute and
3. The two hand finger analysis

Repetition = Memorization. On every page, you will find a discussion of one of the foundations of salvation which are written in different contexts. You will find concepts about Church history, the oneness of God, the three manifestations of one God, three persons of one God, the Trinity, the Deity of Jesus Christ, meaning Jesus is a manifestation of God Himself, the power in God's name, the method of salvation, and how to be "born again," repeated over and over and over again. This repetition = memorization concept is referred to in my first book as "the jazz of writing". In this book, you will see the "same salad; different dressing".

In addition, upon the completion of the book, you will see based on church history, there really is a conspiracy against "understanding" the oneness of God and the conspiracy against Jesus Christ and the Christian Church. We have been deceived so long about the Deity of Jesus Christ that when the truth and the oneness of God's nature are revealed it seems to be sacrilege.

Even though, the truths we will discover will be painful to our understanding, our traditions, and our own beliefs, the truth of the gospel of Jesus Christ must be revealed. And that truth will be revealed in this book by understanding the conspiracy of wickedness in high places.

"Jesus is Lord (Yeshua is Yahweh)"
(Gen. 17:1, Deut. 6:4, Isa. 9:6, 43:11, Luke 2:11,
John 1:10, 8:24, 58, Titus 2:13, Rev. 1:7-8)

CHAPTER 1

THE CONSPIRACY OF WICKEDNESS IN HIGH PLACES

We have seen over the years that Christianity and the name of Jesus Christ are not being mentioned in public as often as they were in the past. And in the last few years we have been hearing more about the persecution of Christians around the world. We can clearly see there is a worldwide conspiracy against the name of Jesus Christ and the Christian Church.

Review: Biblical Banners Banned Under Friday Night Lights. Orlando Sentinel, October 5, 2012, pg. A-15.

Review: Report: 100 million Christians Persecuted, Orlando Sentinel, January 9, 2013, pg. A4.

Review: Rollins Boots Religious Group, Says it Violates Anti-Bias Policy, Orlando Sentinel, March 8, 2013, section B, Rollins College versus religious liberty? March 19, 2013.

Review: "Step-on-"Jesus": Outcry Misses Lesson's Point," Orlando Sentinel, March 28, 2013, sec. B.

Review: Case may curb prayers that start meetings. Orlando Sentinel, May 27, 2013, front page.

The purpose of this book is to inform Christians of conspiracies against them, conspiracies against "understanding" the oneness of God, and a conspiracy against the Christian church; starting with church history at the Nicene Council of 325AD.

In addition, there are conspiracies that will affect Christians worldwide and these conspiracies are slowly and secretively transforming the lives of people of the world into a one world government, which according to prophecy will dominate and control people by labeling every person with the mark of the beast on the hand or forehead.

I have never seen so many conspiracy theories in the news, which are prophecies coming true. We can see prophecies unfolding right before our eyes. (Compare events in the news media and prophecies in the Holy Bible).

To understand the conspiracies we will discuss, you will need to understand the definition of conspiracy according to an excerpt from Dictionary.com.

con·spir·a·cy

noun, plural-cies.

1. the act of conspiring
2. an evil, unlawful, treacherous, or surreptitious plan formulated in secret by two or more persons; plot.
3. a combination of persons for a secret, unlawful, or evil purpose: He joined the conspiracy to overthrow the government.
4. Law. an agreement by two or more persons to commit a crime, fraud, or other wrongful act
5. Any concurrence in action; combination in bringing about a given result.

Now, let's take a look at what Wikipedia says about this "new world order".

"The common theme in conspiracy theories about a new world order is that a secretive power elite with a globalist agenda is conspiring to eventually rule the world through an authoritarian world government—which replaces sovereign nation-state—and an all-encompassing propaganda

2

that ideologizes its establishment as the culmination of history's progress. Significant occurrences in politics and finance are speculated to be orchestrated by an unduly influential cabal operating through many front organizations. Numerous historical and current events are seen as steps in an on-going plot to achieve world domination through secret political gatherings and decision-making processes".

Some believe the biggest conspiracy we have recently seen is the speech by our former President George. H. W. Bush about the new world order. However, I submit to you this speech is not the biggest conspiracy. The conspiracy against understanding the oneness of God and the conspiracy against Jesus Christ and the Christian Church really is the biggest conspiracy (research: George H. W. Bush and the New World Order).

In his speech on September 11, 1990, during a joint session of the Congress, President Bush warned of a coming new world order that will be successful, and he indicated he is a part of this new world order. President Bush again mentioned the new world order in his State of the Union address in 1991.

As Christians, we know this new world order as our dollar bill suggests, is a system to control all political, religious, military, traffic, law enforcement, medical and financial organizations of the world under one all seeing eye, which will be controlled by one man: the Antichrist.

This conspiracy/prophecy has already been foretold in the Bible, and we are seeing it happening right before our eyes. The conspiracy theories I'm most concerned about are those that relate to the works of the Antichrist and population control.

The new world order is not only a conspiracy; it's prophecy that will come true. President Bush was correct when he warned us "we will be successful". Who are we?

We are the world leaders who have put together a system to control the world, its finances and its peoples. Go to any major search engine and put in the search box the name of any world leader plus the phrase, "and the new world order". You will be shocked at how your eyes will be opened to a new reality.

I'm going to show you how, as a Christian, you have unknowingly participated in a conspiracy against understanding the oneness of God and the elaborate manmade (Satan influenced) conspiracy against Jesus Christ and the Christian Church. Today, Christians are still making socially accepted antichrist statements against Jesus Christ and the Christian Church which will be revealed in this book.

I have found, the best way to keep a conspiracy secret is to talk about it openly. Let's take a look at some examples of how conspiracies are talked about openly in books, the news, and on the internet. The following are some books about these worldwide conspiracies.

- Tragedy and Hope A History of the World in our Time by Carroll Quigley

- 63 Documents the Government doesn't Want you to Read by Jesse Ventura.

- Cruel and Unusual: Bush/Cheney's New World Order by Mark Chrispin Miller.

- New World Order, The Ancient Plans of Secret Societies by William T. Still.

- Illuminati: The Cult that Hijacked the World by Henry Makow, Ph.D.

- The Secret Destiny of America by Manly P. Hall.

- The Brotherhood of Darkness by Dr. Stanley Monteith.

- The True Story of the Bilderberg Group by Daniel Estulin.

- The Trillion Dollar Conspiracy and How the New World Order, Man-made Diseases and Zombie Banks are Destroying America, by Jim Marrs.

- The Fearful Master, A Second Look at the United Nations, by G. Edward Griffin

Don't think for a moment that your vote for either a Republican or Democrat will somehow cause us to escape this new world order. Your choice of candidates won't stop nor hinder this sinister plot against the world. Former president Bill Clinton indicated the Republicans and Democrats are in favor of this coming new world order.

On the Sid Roth Show, with Shane Warren, June 25-29, 2012. show 1806. Reference: Matthew 16 (www sidroth.org). Warren said, "The church has become so religious that we cannot discern the signs of the times. The signs of the time are upon this generation and they can't see it. The scripture said there is blindness upon the people, and they are not discerning".

Roth said, "The scriptures talk about a blindness on the eyes of the Jewish people as to who Jesus is, but what you are describing is there is a blindness of people who call themselves Christian".

If Christians will open their spiritual eyes, they will be able to see, there is a convergence of numerous conspiracies that have become prophecies being fulfilled in our lifetime. Once we research these conspiracies, we will understand the scripture that says, there is spiritual wickedness in high places (Ephesians 5:8-16, 6:12). When God open your eyes, you will be able to see how the satanic forces in the world have come together to destroy the world as we know it. And we can see it in the news media.

"Jesus is Lord (Yeshua is Yahweh)"
(Gen. 17:1, Deut. 6:4, Isa. 9:6, 43:11, Luke 2:11,
John 1:10, 8:24, 58, Titus 2:13, Rev. 1:7-8)

Chapter 2

Conspiracies in the News Media

The following are some examples of conspiracies that are in the news and are early developments of prophecies that we can understand from a Christian perspective. We can now see this new world order is not so secret anymore because President George H. W. Bush, Jesse Ventura and Alex Jones have opened our eyes. The world is now at a point where this new world order cannot be stopped. Why? It's prophecy.

Malachi Martin, in his book The Keys of This Blood presents an article that says, "One World System Coming".

> *"Willing or not, ready or not, we are all involved....The competition is about who will establish the first one-world system of government that has ever existed in the society of nations. It is about who will hold and wield the dual power of authority and control over each of us as individuals and over all of us together as a community....*
>
> *Our way of life as individuals and as citizens of the nations; our families and our jobs; our trade and commerce and money; our educational systems and our religions and our cultures; even the badges of our national identity; which most of us have always taken for granted---all will have been powerfully and radically*

altered forever. No one can be exempted from its effects. No sector of our lives will remain untouched".

There was another article by the Associated Press ("UN Summit Ready for New World Order") that was carried by the *Birmingham News,* on January 31, 1992"

"Leaders of the Security Council nations were in New York today for their first summit, ready to place the United Nations at the center of a new world order and forge a common policy on peacemaking and arms control...

The gathering of leaders of the 15 Security Council nations marks the first time since the founding of the world organization in 1945 that the council, the most powerful U. N. body, has convened at the highest level".

Now let's take a look at some conspiracies of the new world order that are not so secret anymore. Do your own research using the following names or terms. At the end of each name or phrase add the term "and the new world order".

President George H. W. Bush, Jesse Ventura, Alex Jones, population control, United Nations, the United Nations water rights, Agenda 21, The Council on Foreign Wars, The Pope, The U. S. One Dollar Bill, 9/11/2001, Chemtrails, U.N. agency: Tainted air is human carcinogen – Orlando Sentinel October 18, 2013, The Federal Reserve (is not a governmental agency and is privately owned?), North American Union, World Banks (cashless society?), Federal Drug Administration (FDA), Pharmaceutical Companies, flu vaccinations, CO2=PSEC, FEMA (concentration camps?), The Monsanto Corp., Trilateral Commission, Corporate logos, National ID card, The Patriot Act, NSA, Gun Control, Microchips, World Health Organizations, the New National Health care Law (the RFID Chip–HR 3962), Secret Societies, Communism, Dwight D. Eisenhower, Abraham Lincoln, John F. Kennedy (the Presidents who told the truth), Martin Luther King, and the entertainment industry (satanic worship–young entertainers-early deaths?).

In addition, the following conspiracies are found in our Newspapers and should cause alarm for mankind worldwide not just in the United States. The best kept worldwide secrets are the ones that can be seen as being unbelievable. The following conspiracies are unbelievable and can be seen.

Research: Monsanto Corp. GMOs, Wheat eaters reap host of problems, Orlando Sentinel Feb. 18, 2013, pg. A6, Monsanto protesters gather at City Hall, Orlando Sentinel, May 26, 2013, Pg. B3, U.S. finds unapproved modified wheat in Ore, Orlando Sentinel, May 30, 2013, page A4)

Research: Prescription drugs are killing more people than illegal drugs and car accidents. Tainted medications are actually causing dreaded diseases. (Orlando Sentinel, FOX 10 News) (Population Control?).

Research: More Meningitis deaths tied to steroid injections, Orlando Sentinel October 6, pg. B3, October 7, 2012 pg. A-4. (Population Control?) Infowars.com.

Research: 9 polio health workers shot to death in Nigeria, Orlando Sentinel, Saturday, Feb. 9, 2013. (Distrust of worldwide vaccinations– population control?) ($CO2=PSEC$?) Infowars.com.

Research: Drug warnings expanded in meningitis outbreak, Orlando Sentinel, Oct. 27, 2012, Front Page (Population Control?).

Research: Experts urge vaccination as flu season makes early start. Orlando Sentinel January 9, 2013, pg. B-5, (Population Control?) ($CO2=PSEC$?) Infowars.com.

Research: Vaccines to help poor girls in African and Asia, Orlando Sentinel, Feb. 4, 2013, pg. A7. (Is this a step toward depopulation and sterilizations of the poor in Africa and Asia?) ($CO2=PSEC$?) prisonplanet.com. (Population Control?)

Research: Tainted baby food and baby products (BPA/BHT?) California move could limit use of toxic flame retardants, Orlando Sentinel, Saturday Feb. 9, 2013 pg. A6. (Population Control?)

Research: The dangers of fluoride. Why is fluoride in our drinking water? What is the real truth? Does toothpaste with fluoride prevent tooth decay or cause tooth decay? Does fluoride cause sicknesses and death? **Stop fluoridating our water,** Orlando Sentinel, June 10, 2013 A3 (Population Control?).

Research the dangers of fluoride and children. Orlando Sentinel January 9, 2013, front page

Orange bucks child dental health trends that earned Florida a "D,". Why would they put dangerous fluoride treatments on low income children's teeth? Harvard study confirms fluoride causes brain damage and reduced IQ in children. Fluoride is extremely dangerous even in small amounts, (Population Control?).

Research: Contamination (toxic) seafood from polluted waters in third world countries is being sold to American Consumers (Reference: toxic food imports).

Research: What are the dangers of CFL light bulbs – commercial and residential (curly top bulbs?) Why do we put these dangerous bulbs in our home? If they break, they will cause in most cases, contamination of the whole house through the air conditioner and/or heating units. (Population Control?),

Research: The dangers of a cashless society. Direct deposits, debit and credit cards are some of the destructive tenets of the new world order wherein no physical money will be used to buy or sell. All money and assets will be controlled by banks and private financial institutions by computer key strokes. Banks will take assets away from families (heirs) and the elderly. (Reverse Mortgage?). Purpose: To re - enslave the population with massive amounts of debt. (Research: the Real ID Act: President Ronald Reagan hated it).

Research: The dangers of scanning and face recognition equipment which could be used to read imbedded microchips or tattoos implanted on the forehead or on the hand. Without the mark (chip, tattoo, or some identifying mark), you won't be able to buy nor sell anything. Your chip or some identifying mark could be cut off by the bank. Physical money is slowly being eliminated from society. (Revelation 14:9-10, 13:17). (Population Control?)

Research: Presidential Pardons: Why are criminals pardoned? What was their crime? What was the relationship between the person being pardoned and the President of the United States? What was relationship of the person being pardoned and the powerful elite?

Finally, the greatest conspiracy of all is the conspiracy against understanding the oneness of God and against Jesus Christ and the Christian Church.

You will find an antidote for all of these anticipated events by understanding the keys of the kingdom of heaven, the great commission, how to be born again, and how to be washed in the blood of Jesus Christ which is the rock upon which the Church is built. For who is God, save the LORD? and who is a "Rock," save our God? (II Samuel 22:32, I Corinthians 10:4, Matthew 28:19, Luke 16:16, Acts 2:38, Colossians 3:17, I Peter 3:21).

In Matthew 16:18, the keys of the kingdom of heaven are based on the *name* of Jesus Christ who is the Rock upon which the Church is built.

In Matthew 28:19, the great commission is based on the *name* of the Father, Son, and Holy Ghost-Jesus Christ.

In Acts 2:38, John 3:5, How to be born again is based on the *name* of Jesus Christ.

In Acts 4:12, there is no other *name* whereby we must be saved-Jesus Christ. Learn more about the keys and how to be washed in the blood in later chapters.

I realize there will be Christians who will experience a satanic attack of "Fear" but we must understand, God did not give us a spirit of fear.

On Sunday Morning, March 4, 2012, Senior Pastor Michael Williams preached a dynamic sermon called, "The Fearful". Pastor Williams stated;

The overcomers are going to paradise and the next verse says "but the fearful, and unbelieving, and the abominable, and murderers, and whoremongers, and sorcerers, and idolaters, and all liars, shall have their part in the lake which burneth with fire and brimstone which is the second death". It's a heaven or hell issue.

It doesn't mean nothing happened to them, it doesn't mean they were never hurt or push down or knocked out of the way, it doesn't mean they never suffered sickness or setbacks or trouble or trials, it simply means they overcame (fear).

The Bible says, he that overcomes (fear) is the perquisite to paradise. You have got to overcome it (fear).

Nobody is going to paradise unless they overcome (fear). God urges his followers to be not afraid. Let not your hearts be troubled. Fear smothers faith.

Love is perfect and perfect love casteth out fear. God do not want us to be fearful. You have got to overcome it. It's a heaven and hell issue.

God's most common command was to not be afraid. Being fearful and unbelieving is a contradiction of the highest order. You and I must believe Jesus Christ is greater than anything on this earth. It matters to God that we know who he is and what he is. God does not want us be afraid". Yes, it is a heaven and hell issue.

Based on this powerful sermon by Pastor Williams, through whom God spoke, you shouldn't concern yourself with these manmade conspiracy theories, which are prophecies being fulfilled.

We should be more concerned about protecting our family by studying God's Word and understanding how to be washed in the blood of Jesus Christ who is the Saviour of the World. You can escape, God has an open door policy. Seek to find the door and who the door is. This information is for your own research. Review these conspiracy theories but don't waste your time; these things will happen. (Matthew 16:16-19, 28:19, Acts 2:38).

My concern and my goal is to direct your attention to the conspiracy against "understanding" the oneness of God and the Deity of Jesus Christ. Once you understand these conspiracies are real and you can see them, then you will be able to see how conspiracies developed, over time, to include the conspiracy, against Jesus Christ and the Christian Church.

These conspiracies and the misunderstanding of scripture began at the Ecumenical Council of Churches in 325 and 381AD. These Churches took away the concept of the oneness of God and replaced God's oneness with a paganistic/polytheistic Christian theology called, "The Trinity". The "Trinitarian Doctrine" is heresy and is an affront to the very oneness of God as expressed in Deuteronomy 6:4. We have, as Christians, turned to a Paganistic Trinitarian Christianity: (Idol Worship-Pope prays at a statue of Mary) Reference: Orlando Sentinel, 12/10/12 page A9).

"Jesus is Lord (Yeshua is Yahweh)"
(Gen. 17:1, Deut. 6:4, Isa. 9:6, 43:11, Luke 2:11,
John 1:10, 8:24, 58, Titus 2:13, Rev. 1:7-8)

CHAPTER 3

THE CONSPIRACY AT THE ECUMENICAL COUNCIL (325AD)

Conspiracy? Why? To Make a Mockery of God's Oneness (Deuteronomy 6:4). The history of the Christian Church is an area most lay Christians have never studied. The following comments are an attempt to clarify theological discussions and to separate truth from conspiracies, manmade doctrine, assumptions, and misunderstandings of scripture.

Historically, in Christian theology, there has been a conspiracy to demonize the terms; Modalism, Sabellianism, Monarchianism and the Oneness of God starting at the Nicene Council of 325AD. This satanic attack against understanding the oneness of God and the conspiracy against Jesus Christ and the Christian Church has continued to be a factor of misunderstandings in most of our modern day Catholic and Protestant Churches.

In order to understand the oneness of God in the Old Testament and the operations of that same God in the New Testament, one would have to have a working knowledge of Church history. Theological discussions at the Council of Nicea in 325AD and the Council of Constantinople in 381AD were used to prove the doctrine of the Trinity. The following discussions were the main issues discussed at these councils;

(325AD) The first discussion was the relationship between God (the Father) and Jesus Christ (the Son).

Results: God and Jesus are of the same substance–Nicene Creed: "True God of True God".

(325AD) What day of the week would the Christian Church, worship God?

Results: Changed the Sabbath Day-Saturday to Sunday.

(325AD) What day of the week would the Christian Church celebrate Easter (a pagan holiday)?

Results: Easter will be celebrated on Sunday.

(381AD) What is the relationship between God (the Father), Jesus Christ (the Son), and the Holy Ghost (Spirit)?

Results: God is three persons in one God which is of the same substance.

The purpose of these results is to simplify the theological debates and the terms used during these early years-(100-381AD). We have to understand how the results from these councils affect modern day Christians' understanding of the oneness of God. There were three major understandings of the oneness of God that came out of these Councils. They were;

1. **Trinitarian Christianity** (Constantine's Roman Catholic Ecumenical Council of Churches–a manmade doctrine of men– three persons in one God). Two of the main scriptures used to validate the Trinitarian position were Genesis 1:26 and John 1:1.

   Trinitarians believe in the philosophy of three distinct persons who are co-equal, co-eternal, and agree in one essence of one God. The Trinitarian doctrine is a doctrine developed and put together by men so they could have a doctrine that would be agreeable to all the various Bishops and a doctrine that would be acceptable to the emperor Constantine. Constantine was not concerned about doctrine; he was more concerned about the stability of his kingdom. In other words, stop the bickering about the relationship between Jesus Christ and the Father and come to some type of agreement. Finally, the Trinitarian Doctrine was agreed upon by the majority of the bishops at the Council of Constantinople 381AD. The separation of persons, Father and Son was of the same substance was agreed upon in 325AD. And the doctrine of three persons of the same substance agreeing in one God which included the Holy Ghost was clarified in 381AD at Constantinople. There were other councils that followed, but these two councils were the beginnings of three distinct but co-equal, co-eternal substances of one God.

This new Christian Trinitarian doctrine of the Roman Catholic Ecumenical Council of Churches spread throughout the Christian world and was not challenged by the Eastern Orthodox, Anglicans, Oriental Orthodox, Assyrian Church of the East, Lutherans, nor Calvinists. The Trinitarian Doctrine embraced by these historical churches, in my opinion, is one of the greatest falling away from the gospel of Jesus Christ the world has ever known (II Thessalonians 2:3, I Timothy 4:1-2).

The Ecumenical Council of Bishops decided; if any doctrine was not the Trinitarian doctrine, then that doctrine is false and heretical. The Trinitarian doctrine of three persons ruled over scripture (Deuteronomy 6:4, John 10:30, Hebrews 1:3, 8).

In addition any priest who would disagree with this new doctrine was ostracized or killed. Again, the Trinitarian doctrine is a doctrine made by men and endorsed by the Emperor Constantine, a pagan (Colossians 2:8-12).

According to the book, "What's Behind the New World Order? How it will Affect you! Published in 1991 by Inspiration Books,

> *"The nominal conversion of the Roman Emperor Constantine, in the early part of the fourth century, caused great rejoicing and the world, cloaked with a form of righteousness walked into the church. Paganism, while appearing to be vanquished, became the conqueror. Pagan doctrines, ceremonies, and superstitions were incorporated into the faith and worship of the professed followers of Christ, Ibid, pg. 5.*

The Trinity was the unsound pagan doctrine that was introduced by Constantine and the Roman Catholic Ecumenical Council of Churches. The philosophy of three persons in one God is vain, deceitful, a rudiment of this world and a tradition of men and not after Christ. God knows all, therefore, God warns us against this type philosophy and tradition of men which was created at the Nicene Council of 325AD. (Colossians 2:8-12).

2. **Ditheistic/Binitarian/Subordination Christianity** (similar terms of Bishop Marcion and the Arian philosophy – doctrine of men). Two divine beings in one God. According to this philosophy, the Holy Ghost is God's force of nature. This theology uses various New Testament scripture wherein Jesus Christ talks about "His Father" (Matthew 7:21, 10:32, 10:33, 12:50, 16:17, John 14:2, etc). Thus, the Son being subordinate to the Father.

    This type Christian theology believes in one big or major God the Father and one lessor god, Jesus Christ, not of the same substance as God. One God - two Divine beings. Reference: Jehovah's Witnesses article, "What Does the Bible Really Teach?" pgs 42, 203.

    For example, in "The "New World Translation of the Holy Scriptures," a translation used by the Jehovah's Witnesses as their Bible, John 1:1 is used to indicate a lessor god with the small "g". Furthermore, Ditheistic and Binitarian Christians are closely related to Subordination Christians who believe Jesus Christ is subordinate to God the Father.

3. **Oneness Christianity.** This is the doctrine of the Apostles which closely resembled Modalism, Sabellianism and Monarchianism. Oneness Pentecostal Christians believe there is only one Person in the Godhead. And that one Person was manifested as the Father, Son, and the Holy Spirit. That one Person in the Godhead is Jesus Christ according to scripture (Deuteronomy 6:4, Isaiah 9:6, Matthew 1:21-23, John 14:6-9, 10:30, 33, 8:24, 58, Philippians 2:10-11, Colossians 1:14-19, 2:8-9, I Timothy 3:16, Titus 2:13, Jude 1:25, Revelation 1:7-8).

Modern day Oneness Apostolic Pentecostal Christians are strictly monotheistic. We believe there is only one God who was manifested in one Person–Jesus Christ. We also believe the one God in the Old Testament is the same God revealed in the New Testament as the Son of God, the Word who is Jesus Christ. Jesus Christ in His Spirit form as the Word made the heavens and earth. (John 1:10).

Now, since most Christians believe in the oneness of God, we are going to focus on God's oneness. The following excerpt from www.Wikipedia.com gives us an objective understanding of the debate at the Nicene and Constantinople Councils concerning the oneness of God.

Excerpt: "From Wikipedia, the free encyclopedia

"Oneness Pentecostalism *(also known as Apostolic Pentecostalism or One God Pentecostalism) refers to a grouping of denominations and believers within Pentecostal Christianity, of whom subscribe to the nontrinitarian theological doctrine of Oneness. This movement first emerged around 1914 as the result of doctrinal disputes within the nascent Pentecostal movement and claims an estimated 24 million adherents today.*

Oneness Pentecostalism derives its distinctive name from its teaching on the Godhead, which is popularly referred to as the Oneness doctrine. This doctrine states that there is one God, a singular spirit who manifests himself in many different ways, including as Father, Son and Holy Spirit. This stands in sharp contrast to the doctrine of three distinct and eternal "persons" posited by Trinitarian theology. Oneness believers baptize in the name Jesus Christ, commonly referred to as Jesus name baptism, rather than using the Trinitarian formula.

*"**Sabellianism,** (also known as modalism, modalistic monarchianism, or modal monarchism) is the nontrinitarian belief that the Heavenly Father, Resurrected Son and Holy Spirit are different modes or*

aspects of one God, as perceived by the believer, rather than three distinct persons in God Himself. The term Sabellianism comes from Sabellius, a theologian and priest from the third century. Modalism differs from Unitarianism by accepting the Christian doctrine that Jesus was fully God".

It's up to modern day Oneness Apologists to fully embrace the foundations of these theological terms and fine tune the terms so the truth of the oneness of God might be found. These terms have been demonized historically by Catholic and Protestant theology for centuries beginning with the discussions at the Nicene Council 325AD.

During the 4th-5th centuries, Christian terms were used to categorize different religious beliefs of pastors, bishops and apologists. Modalism, Sabellianism, Monarchianism were used for discussions but were later demonized as heretical by the Roman Catholic Ecumenical Council of Churches and their theology because these terms did not include a Trinity nor did they embrace a "Trinitarian Doctrine".

Thus, for centuries these terms Modalism, Sabellianism, and Monarchianism were used by the Roman Catholic Ecumenical Council of Churches (325AD and 381AD) to virtually shut down any search for the truth concerning the oneness of God (Deuteronomy 6:4). It was determined that any terms which did not conform to the Trinity of three persons in one God were deemed heretical by the Nicene Council. Therefore, the foundation of God's Word and the Oneness of God's nature, as expressed in Deuteronomy 6:4, would have been deemed, historically, heretical by this errant council of Bishops.

God's Word is not a three persons in one God theology. How ludicrous for intelligent men to believe in this evil theology of three persons in one God which is polytheism. Any type of Polytheistic or Tritheistic doctrine such as the Trinitarian doctrine is a distraction from the clearer focus of God's

Word concerning his oneness. Modalism, Sabellianism, Monarchianism are similar but should not have any relationship with modern day Oneness Pentecostal Christians. Modalism or modes which were terms used historically for theological discussions by Old Age Catholic Theologians have a solid foundation of truth but these terms are not Biblical. In our effort to understand the conspiracy against the oneness of God and this type of Modalist theology, we would have to separate the terms Modalism and Oneness Pentecostal Christians.

"Jesus is Lord (Yeshua is Yahweh)"
(Gen. 17:1, Deut. 6:4, Isa. 9:6, 43:11, Luke 2:11,
John 1:10, 8:24, 58, Titus 2:13, Rev. 1:7-8)

CHAPTER 4

MODALISM VS ONENESS PENTECOSTAL CHRISTIANS

The conspiracy against the oneness of God was planted by Satan using the terms modes or Modalism which were demonized at the Nicene Council (325AD). In Oneness Christian Theology, God speaks of Himself as being one, a Person, a form, or manifestations of one God which are Biblical terms as opposed to modes or modalism.

These terms; one, oneness, Person, form, manifestations and the concept of God being one are Biblical and are terms used interchangeably in scripture. God revealed himself in three different forms or manifestations for the salvation of mankind; the Father, the Son, and the Holy Ghost (Matthew 28:19, Philippians 2:6, I Timothy 3:16).

Therefore, to dispense with any misunderstanding of scripture, let's take a look at terms used in the Bible and terms that were not used, Biblically.

1. **Modalism,** Sabellianism, Monarchianism as a description of who God is, are true concepts but they are not Biblical terms.
2. **One Person** is a Biblical term which is true and should be used to describe one God (Job 13:6-11, Hebrews 1:3, 8). The Son is one Person and He is God (Colossians 2:9, Revelation. 1:8).

3. **Forms or Manifestations** of one God are true and are Biblical terms which should be used to describe God. (Philippians 2:6, I Timothy 3:16, I John 1:1-2).
4. **The Oneness of God** is the concept of being "one" which is true and is a Biblical concept of who God is (Deuteronomy 6:4).

Thus, in historical Christianity starting at the Nicene Council; the Catholic Bishops never spoke of God as one Person which they termed heresy, is not true. At these errant councils, God is called, three persons. The three persons in one God is a satanic attacked against the oneness of God and is a conspiracy against the Deity of Jesus Christ and the Christian Church (Deuteronomy 6:4, Luke 2:11, Galatians 1:8-9).

In our search for the oneness of God and the one Person of his nature, we should dispense with the theological name calling. Christians should search for the absolute oneness of God. We should study to show ourselves approved and use the Biblical terms – one, oneness, Person, forms or manifestations of one God in our search for truth. (Job 13:6-11, Hebrews 1:3, I Timothy 3:16, II Timothy 3:16).

Based on all these terms, we have found the Oneness Apostolic Christians who were historically called Modalism, Sabellianism, and Monarchianism were ostracized because of the Catholic and Protestants misunderstandings of the oneness of God.

The Father, the Son, and the Holy Ghost are not modes, as the Roman Catholic Ecumenical Council of Churches suggest because mode is a manmade description and it is not Biblical. Modes when referring to God overshadows the understanding of the oneness of God. God should be referred to as One God, three manifestations or three forms of one God. These are terms used by God to describe Himself in one Person-Jesus Christ. (II Corinthians 5:19, Colossians 1:19, 2:9).

God's Oneness is God's greatest attribute; therefore, God's oneness has come under a satanic attack for centuries of Church history. Research The Trinity.

Satan has cleverly attached these aforementioned terms, specifically modalism, to the concept of the oneness of God to try to discourage the search for the oneness of God's nature by Christians who have a love for truth. Thus far, this satanic conspiracy against the oneness of God, who is Jesus Christ, has had a devastating effect on modern day Christianity (Genesis 17:1, Revelation 1:7-8).

We should insist Christians use the terms one, oneness, Person, revelation, forms, or manifestations of one God which are Biblical terms. Modes, Modalism, Sabellianism, Monarchianism are not Biblical terms when referring to the oneness of God. The terms; Modes, Modalism, Sabellianism, and Monarchianism are true man made understandings of Gods' nature but they should not be used in theological discussions because these terms have been demonized and causes confusion.

The oneness of God must be separated from any terms that will cause confusion because God is not the author of confusion. Only Biblical terms should be used when referring to God.

God is absolutely one Person and that's what we should ascribe to; God's Oneness as it relates to the three manifestations mentioned in scripture. (Genesis 17:1, Revelation 1:7-8, Deuteronomy 6:4, Luke 2:11, Isaiah 9:6, John 1:14, I Timothy 3:16, I John 1:1-2).

Dr. David K. Bernard said in his book, "Oneness and Trinity A.D.100-300. Page 162

> ."*Finally, since we do not know with certainty everything the various Modalists believed, it is not productive to identify modern Oneness directly with ancient modalism, Patripassianism, or Sabellianism. While the basic view of God seems to be fundamentally the same, there is no historical link. It is not appropriate to impute to the modern Oneness movement everything that the Modalists taught or everything that various historians, ancient and modern, have attributed to the Modalists. Oneness Pentecostals today should be evaluated by their own clearly expressed and well-documented position, not by ancient labels that mean different things to different people and that often prejudice people's thinking".*

The revealed truths in this book is an effort to stop the prejudice, the name calling, and the labels which were used by Satan to confuse and separate Christians' search for truth. Christians should search the scriptures to understand the oneness of God and the saving grace of Jesus Christ.

We have to re-establish a platform for theological dialogue among Christians who don't have a hidden agenda but have a burning desire to understand how the Father, the Son, and the Holy Ghost are identified as one God (John 10:30, 33, John 14:6-9, 17-18).

We have come to realize the true gospel of Jesus Christ is not being taught in most of our Christian churches today. These churches don't understand the oneness of God as it was taught by the apostles. The oneness of God is a standalone term meaning God is absolutely one Person. God is one Person on a higher level of intellectual understanding than one would think of in human terms.

In other words, three persons of God is an assumption and cannot be proven. On the other hand, three manifestations and the concept of the oneness of God can be logically proven in scripture. God is absolutely one Person and He is in one Person – Jesus Christ (Job 13:6-11, Hebrews 1:3, 8, II Corinthians 5:19).

Again, for clarification, we should throw out all of our man made definitions and use the Biblical terms such as one, oneness, Person, forms or manifestations of one God. Three manifestations should be used to identify the one God – Jehovah. Jesus Christ is a manifestation, he is not a mode. (John 1:31, I Timothy 3:16, 1 John 1:1-2).

Based on the terms developed during early church history, Peter, Paul and the apostles would have been considered heretics, Modalists or Sabellianists because the apostles believed in the three manifestations (forms) of One God for the salvation of men. Manifestations of God can be proven by the Word of God but three persons of God as stated by the "doctrine of men" at the Council of Constantinople (381AD) is illogical and cannot be proven.

God did not give his mystery to the wise and the prudent; He has given it to babes. Reading the Bible is not so complicated that one has to have a theological degree to understand the truths laced throughout.

Believers who have the gift of the Holy Spirit and with limited education can understand the Word of God, in some cases, better than the educated. Once you try to dissect every Word of God with human logic you will lose the true essence of God and in most cases take the Word of God out of context. True believers who have the Holy Ghost can read the literal Word of God with little or no man made interpretations and get a complete understanding of the gospel of salvation and the oneness of God.

On the other hand, in these end-times, some of the most powerful men in Christendom will be those who have theological degrees and with the power of the Holy Spirit will get a better understanding of the mystery, knowledge, and oneness of God. These highly educated men and women, like the apostle Paul, will be able to bring the world back to the simple truths and understanding of the oneness of God, the gospel message, and the saving grace of Jesus Christ.

Paul was an intelligent man who was highly educated and could explain the gospel to believers who had limited educations. The gospel of Jesus Christ is not complicated to a believer regardless of their education. The gospel becomes complicated when we try to fit it into our own traditions, understandings, and philosophies of men, which try to identify God with the paganistic/polytheistic term three persons. God never told us He is three persons. Three persons is a confusion created by historical writers and scholars who erroneously tried to describe God. This paganistic concept of God was used to appease Constantine and his fellow pagans. "The Trinity" was consistent with the paganistic/polytheistic theology of that era.

In summary, three persons of God cannot be proven scripturally. However, three manifestations of God can be proven and was historically called Modalism. Modalism should not be used to describe the oneness of God. Modalism is a manmade term that has been demonized by the council of Bishops in 325AD. Study other false religions that have a Trinity of three deities in one God and you will find they are Trinitarian (for example: Egyptian and Hindu gods - The Trinity).

In order to understand the oneness of God we will have to understand the conspiracy against Jesus Christ and the church.

"Jesus is Lord (Yeshua is Yahweh)"
(Gen. 17:1, Deut. 6:4, Isa. 9:6, 43:11, Luke 2:11,
John 1:10, 8:24, 58, Titus 2:13, Rev. 1:7-8)

CHAPTER 5

THE CONSPIRACY AGAINST JESUS CHRIST AND THE CHURCH

If we want to follow the Spirit of truth, which is Christianity, there must be another revolutionary change to our Christian experience. Christians, must come back to the "Shema," "Hear, O Israel: The Lord our God is one Lord:" (Deuteronomy 6:4),

In order to understand the "Shema" and the oneness of God, we must get to know Jesus Christ as the one Lord God Almighty (Isaiah 9:6, Luke 2:11, Titus 2:13, Jude 1:25, Revelation 1:7-8).

We must have a paradigm shift which reveals a clearly defined level of truth in the humanity and Deity of Jesus Christ, whose name is translated Jehovah Saviour-God with us (Isaiah 43:10-12, Matthew 1:21-23).

G.C.F. Grumbine said in, "The Secret Doctrine of the Order of Melchizedek in the Bible,"

> *""The church will not wholly pass away. What will and must die in ecclesiastical institutions is that which limits man's freedom to know the truth".*

Ellen G. White said; Churches must leave their traditions and false notions and open up their understanding to an evolving truth. (Reference; "The Present Truth," by E.G. White, SDA)

In these last days, God is once again revealing his truths, the power of his name and the Oneness of his nature to the world.

For centuries we have not known we were in error of the true understanding of Christian theology because of our unbelief, disobedience, and lack of knowledge of the Deity of our Lord and Saviour Jesus Christ.

Since the beginning of the Christian Church there has been a concerted effort by Satan to keep the whole world blinded to the truth of God's Word and the saving grace of Jesus Christ through a "bewilderment of the Trinitarian doctrine," a term coined by Bishop Billy G. Newton, Diocesan of the 29th Episcopal District, Pentecostal Assemblies of the World, Inc., and Pastor of The Word of God Church, Orlando, Fla.

The bewilderment of Church doctrine and the conspiracy against the gospel of Jesus Christ were encountered by Paul and the apostles. During his ministry, Paul realized there were others who weren't teaching the same gospel he was teaching the saints. Paul was so concerned about this perversion of the gospel that he said if we or an angel from heaven preach any other gospel; let him be accursed (Galatians 1:6-9).

Today, in most of our Christian churches, we are not teaching the same gospel Paul taught because we have been blinded by a false church doctrine. This false doctrine of the Trinity was first developed at the Council of Nicaea 325AD and was not the doctrine Paul taught the saints. (II Thessalonians 1:7-9).

Satan's deception doesn't necessarily mean he is trying to deceive Christians. Satan is trying to deceive the whole world including Jews, Christians, Muslims and others through a "bewilderment" of a destructive doctrine called, The Trinity, which no one fully understands.

Historical Church doctrine is a conspiracy to destroy the doctrine of the One God, Jesus Christ and the Christian Church. Jesus told Peter the gospel will be built upon a Rock and the gates of hell shall not prevail against it. You are going to be excited to get a full explanation of how the church is built upon the rock (name) of Jesus Christ, how the keys of the kingdom of heaven were used, how to be born again, and how the great commission was carried out by the apostles. We know about the conspiracy against Jesus Christ but there is also a conspiracy against the Christian Church. (Psalm 18:31, Matthew 16:18-19, 28:19, Acts 2:38, 19:1-5).

The conspiracy against the Christian Church is caused by the traditions and philosophies of men and their disobedience to the Word of God. Disobedience comes when we won't study nor try to understand the gospel of Jesus Christ. To understand the gospel message and how we have been disobedient, we must first understand Judaism, their customs, and their culture in the Old Testament/Tanakh.

Judaism is based on the oneness of God, repentance, and blood sacrifice. God has always used the power of his name and the blood sacrifice of a lamb, bullock, turtle dove, etc. for forgiveness of sins. When we look back at the exodus of the children of Israel, we will see God sent the death angel to kill all of the first born of Egypt because the Pharaoh would not let the children of Israel go. If the children of Israel did not follow God's words precisely they would surely die.

God told his people to sprinkle the blood of a pure lamb over the door posts and the death angel will pass over that house. In the New Testament, when we are baptized in God's name, Jesus Christ, our sins are forgiven (passed over) and God doesn't see our sins because our sins are covered by the blood of the Lamb (Acts 2:38, I Peter 3:21 Romans 6:3-4, Ephesians 4:5, Colossians 2:9-12).

The whole gospel message is the death, burial, and resurrection of Jesus Christ and that culmination was carried out in the book of Acts when Peter used the keys of the kingdom of heaven to open the door to the church. (Matthew 16:18-19, 28:19, Acts 2:38).

Christians don't want to deliberately disobey God. They feel they are living as close to God as they know how. I want to assure you in these last days God is opening up the understanding of his Word to those believers who are sincerely seeking to have a closer relationship with him. Let me give you some examples of the disobedience and philosophy of men which are the wilderness of misunderstanding and disobedience.

The following statements are taken out of context and it causes misunderstanding, disobedience, and a conspiracy against the Words of Jesus Christ and the Christian Church. Any suggestion baptism is not necessary is a direct violation of the Words of Jesus Christ and it is a conspiracy to push sinners in the wrong direction (Mark 16:16). Let's take a look at a conspiracy used by Satan to distort the gospel of salvation. Based on our traditional training, the following revelations are absolutely shocking!!!

This is the conspiracy against Salvation: "Confess with your mouth and believe in your heart the Lord Jesus and you are saved" (Romans 10:9).

This scripture is used by modern day churches to explain to repentant sinners seeking salvation they are saved by repeating these words. This could not be further from the truth. Romans 10:9 is one of the scriptures taken out of context.

This scripture is referring to the brethren. We can see they are the brethren by looking at the beginning of the chapter. (Romans 10:1). The brethren are those who have already repented, been baptized in the name of Jesus Christ, and have received the gift of the Holy Spirit according to Peter's sermon in Acts 2:38.

We are in the bewilderment of our own thinking because Jesus Christ said, "He that believeth and is baptized shall be saved; but he that believeth not shall be damned". This scripture, in Romans, is prophetic but its erroneously used because it doesn't take into consideration Matthew 28:19, John 3:5, nor Acts 2:38. Romans 10:9 doesn't mention water and Spirit. Therefore, we have been disobedient because we have not followed the gospel (Matthew 28:19, Mark 16:16, John 3:5, Acts 2:38, II Thessalonians 1:7-12).

The only thing Paul is saying in this scripture is this; since the brethren have already repented, they had been baptized in the name of Jesus Christ, and they have received the Holy Ghost, all they have to do is to have faith and confess it with their mouth the Lord Jesus Christ and believe in their heart God has raised him from the dead, they shall be saved. To understand Romans 10:9, you must understand how to glorify and confess the name of Jesus Christ according to Acts 2:38. To understand salvation in Acts 2:38; lets' bring your attention back to the oneness of God (Shema) with an overview of God in the Old Testament (Isaiah) and the manifestation of Jesus Christ, as God, in the New Testament (John). Thus we will understand how they had to confess the name and its relationship to Matthew 28:19.

"Jesus is Lord (Yeshua is Yahweh)"
(Gen. 17:1, Deut. 6:4, Isa. 9:6, 43:11, Luke 2:11,
John 1:10, 8:24, 58, Titus 2:13, Rev. 1:7-8)

CHAPTER 6

ISAIAH AND JOHN AGREE JESUS CHRIST IS GOD

The best way we can understand the oneness of God and the conspiracy against the name of Jesus Christ is by putting the Old and New Testament together.

One of the greatest prophets in the Old Testament to understand Jesus Christ as God, the Father, the Son, and the Holy Ghost was Isaiah, even though, Isaiah didn't know the name of the Messiah.

In support of the Old Testament, the greatest apostle in the New Testament to understand the Deity of Jesus Christ as God, the Father, the Son, and the Holy Ghost, was the apostle John.

We can say without question the prophet Isaiah and the apostle John agree Jesus Christ is a manifestation of God Himself; one God and one Person of God.

Isaiah and John are by no means all of the books in the Bible that can be compared to reveal the Deity of Jesus Christ. The comparison of Isaiah and John further clarifies the Oneness of God. Jesus Christ is Lord (Yeshua HaMashiach is Yahweh) (Deuteronomy 6:4, Isaiah 9:6, Luke 2:11).

For more comparison scriptures in the Old and New Testaments read my book, "Understanding" The Trinity, Three Persons vs Three Manifestations.

Prophet Isaiah-Old Testament Prophecy		Apostle John-New Testament Revelation	
Isaiah 9:6	God will be born as a man	John 1:10	(Jesus-Yeshua is Yahweh)
Isaiah 9:6	Jesus is the mighty God	John 1:10	(Jesus-Yeshua is Yahweh)
Isaiah 9:6	God/Son/Spirit made Flesh	John 1:14	(Jesus-Yeshua is Yahweh)
Isaiah 9:6	Jesus is the everlasting Father	John 14:6-9	(Jesus-Yeshua is Yahweh)
Isaiah 40:3	A highway for our God	John 1:23	(Jesus-Yeshua is Yahweh)
Isaiah 41:4	Jesus is I am he	John 8:24	(Jesus-Yeshua is Yahweh)
Isaiah 42:5	God created the heaven and earth	John 1:10	(Jesus-Yeshua is Yahweh)
Isaiah 42:8	I will not give my glory to another	John 16:14	(Jesus-Yeshua is Yahweh)
Isaiah 42:8	God will glorify himself in Christ	John 17:1	(Jesus-Yeshua is Yahweh)
Isaiah 43:11	Beside me there is no saviour	John 4:42	(Jesus-Yeshua is Yahweh)
Isaiah 43:12	I am is Jesus Christ	John 8:58	(Jesus-Yeshua is Yahweh)
Isaiah 44:6	Beside me there is no God	John 10:30, 33	(Jesus-Yeshua is Yahweh)
Isaiah 44:8	God doesn't know of any other God	John 1:10, 30	(Jesus-Yeshua is Yahweh)
Isaiah 44:24	The Lord that maketh all things	John 1:1-3, 10	(Jesus-Yeshua is Yahweh)
Isaiah 45:5	There is no God beside me	John 10:30, 33	(Jesus-Yeshua is Yahweh)

Isaiah 45:18	The Lord created the heaven and earth	John 1:1-14	(Jesus-Yeshua is Yahweh)
Isaiah 45:21	A just God and a Saviour	John 4:42	(Jesus-Yeshua is Yahweh)
Isaiah 48:11	I will not give my glory to another	John 12:23	(Jesus-Yeshua is Yahweh)
Isaiah 48:11	I will not give my glory to another	John 13:31-32	(Jesus-Yeshua is Yahweh)
Isaiah 48:11	I will not give my glory to another	John 17:1	(Jesus-Yeshua is Yahweh)
Isaiah 48:12	I am he	John 8:24	(Jesus-Yeshua is Yahweh)
Isaiah 52:6	I am he	John 13:19	(Jesus-Yeshua is Yahweh)

The one Lord God Almighty mentioned in the Old Testament in his Spirit form as the Word is the same God manifested in the form of a man in the New Testament (John 1:14).

Dr. David Bernard shows in his book, *"The Oneness of God,"* the dual nature of Jesus Christ. Dr. Bernard shows Jesus Christ is one God in Spirit and the same God in Flesh (Revelation 1:7-8) pg 86.

Let me give you a simplistic understanding of the oneness of God using a natural phenomenon. Water has three forms or can be manifested in three ways; liquid, solid, steam=the same water. Now, think of God as three forms or manifestations of one God; the Father, Son, and Holy Spirit=the same God. (Deuteronomy 6:4, Isaiah 9:6, Luke 2:11, John 10:30, 33, 14:9, Philippians 2:6, I Timothy 3:16, Hebrews 1:8, I John 1:1-2, Revelation 1:7-8).

Now, let's prove the natural understanding of the properties of water and how this analogy could relate to a Spiritual form of one God.

God the Father	Spirit	liquid	water	Isaiah 9:6
Jesus Christ	the Son	Flesh	Ice (same water)	Matthew 1:21-23
Jesus Christ	the Holy Ghost	Spirit	Steam (same water)	John 14:16-18

We can see from this analogy the three properties of water can be used to understand the three manifestations of one God. The one God in the Old Testament is the same God in the New Testament. God manifested Himself by going from Spirit to Flesh and back to Spirit. There is only one God who is our Lord and Saviour Jesus Christ (Isaiah 43:10-12, Revelation 1:7-8). Jesus Christ is God himself because God said, in the Old Testament, "I will not give my glory to another" (Isaiah 42:8).

"Jesus is Lord (Yeshua is Yahweh)"
(Gen. 17:1, Deut. 6:4, Isa. 9:6, 43:11, Luke 2:11,
John 1:10, 8:24, 58, Titus 2:13, Rev. 1:7-8)

CHAPTER 7

I WILL NOT GIVE MY GLORY TO ANOTHER

There is a conspiracy Jesus Christ does not have the glory of the Father. Let's prove God's Word is true based on the New Testament and his manifestation as Jesus Christ (Colossians 2:9, II Corinthians 5:19). The following scriptures will prove without question God only gives His glory to Himself-Jesus Christ.

Foundational scripture Isaiah 42:8 I am the LORD that is my name and my glory will I not give to another, neither my praise to graven images.

Mark 8:38 Whosoever therefore shall be ashamed of me and of my words in this adulterous and sinful generation; of him also shall the Son of man be ashamed, when he cometh in the glory of his Father with the holy angels. (Jesus Christ is the one God who is glorified-Yeshua is Yahweh).

John 11:4 When Jesus heard that, he said, This sickness is not unto death, but for the glory of God, that the Son of God might be glorified thereby. (Jesus Christ is the one God who is glorified-Yeshua is Yahweh).

John 14:13 And whatsoever ye shall ask in my name, that will I do, that the Father may be glorified in the Son. (Jesus Christ is the one God who is glorified-Yeshua is Yahweh).

John 16:14 He shall glorify me: for he shall receive of mine, and shall shew it unto you. (Jesus Christ is the one God who is glorified-Yeshua is Yahweh).

John 17:1. These words spake Jesus, and lifted up his eyes to heaven, and said, Father, the hour is come; glorify thy Son, that the Son also may glorify thee: (Jesus Christ is the one God who is glorified-Yeshua is Yahweh).

John 17:5 And now, O Father, glorify thou me with thine own self with the glory which I had with thee before the world was. (Jesus Christ is the one God who is glorified-Yeshua is Yahweh).

John 17:24 Father, I will that they also, whom thou hast given me, be with me where I am; that they may behold my glory, which thou hast given me: for thou lovedst me before the foundation of the world. (Jesus Christ is the one God who is glorified-Yeshua is Yahweh).

Jude 1:25 To the only wise God our Saviour, be glory and majesty, dominion and power, both now and for ever. Amen. (Jesus Christ is the one God who is glorified-Yeshua is Yahweh).

Revelation 5:12 Saying with a loud voice, Worthy is the Lamb that was slain to receive power, and riches, and wisdom, and strength, and honour, and glory and blessings. (Jesus Christ is the one God who is glorified-Yeshua is Yahweh).

We can see from the scriptures God has glorified himself in one body and in one Person-Jesus Christ. God has given John a revelation most Christians read yet they don't understand. Now we know for a surety God is one in nature and his Highest and most glorious name is Jesus Christ. (Deuteronomy 6:4, Luke 2:11).

Finally, based on the Word of God, we can understand the oneness of God and how the conspiracy against Jesus Christ and the Christian Church has been revealed

We are all seeking for the truth of the oneness of God by understanding the apostles' doctrine and the manifestations of the one God through Jesus

Christ in the New Testament. Going back we can see people who glorified and worshipped God in the Old Testament. Going forward we see people who worshipped Jesus as the one God Almighty in the New Testament;

Matthew 2:11	They worshipped him	Jesus is Lord (Yeshua is Yahweh)
Matthew 14:33, 28:17	They worshipped him	Jesus is Lord (Yeshua is Yahweh)
Matthew 15:25	She worshipped him	Jesus is Lord (Yeshua is Yahweh)
Luke 24:52	They worshipped him	Jesus is Lord (Yeshua is Yahweh)
John 9:38	He worshipped him	Jesus is Lord (Yeshua is Yahweh)
Hebrews 1:6	Angels of God worship him	Jesus is Lord (Yeshua is Yahweh)

Worshipping the Lord Jesus Christ was not a violation of scripture because God was in Christ reconciling the world unto himself. God will not give his glory to another. Jesus Christ is God himself.

There is a misunderstanding among the Jews and Christians as to the Deity and Lordship of Jesus Christ. Some Christians have a problem believing Jesus Christ was the Spirit of God and was the same God in the Old Testament before he was manifested in the flesh in the New Testament (Genesis 17:1, Revelation 1:7-8). For example, when God speaks, does he mean there is one Lord in the Old Testament and one Lord in the New Testament? Are there two Lords or could Jesus Christ be that one Lord in both the Old and New Testament? Let's take a few scriptures and put them together so we can at least show the Jews that Christians believe in Deuteronomy 6:4. Oneness Christians believe Jesus Christ is the one Lord who is identified in both the Old and New Testaments (I Corinthians 10:4).

Christians believe the one Lord of heaven and earth, whom the Jews believe in; came down from heaven and made himself a body which was in the form of a man (Jesus Christ) the one Lord of the Old Testament (Word).

God calls his incarnation in the Flesh, "his Son" in the New Testament (Matthew 3:16, Hebrews 1:3, 8).

God manifested himself by going from Spirit (Word) to Flesh (Son), then back into a Spiritual form (Holy Ghost) that took the shape of a body. That body or the appearance of a body will be seen at the second coming in all of his splendor and glory.

God incorporated his Spirit into the body of Jesus Christ. Jesus Christ comes in the volume of a book and it's proven throughout both the Old and New Testaments. There is only one Lord and Saviour in both the Old and New Testaments and his name is; our Lord and Saviour Jesus Christ.

Let's put some scriptures together to show the dramatic effect of how God proves he is one Lord in the Spirit, as the Father, in the Old Testament and he is the same Lord manifested, as the Son, in the New Testament. (Colossians 2:9).

Old Testament: Isaiah 9:6. For unto us a child is born, unto us a son is given: and the government shall be upon his shoulder: and his name shall be called Wonderful, Counsellor, The mighty God, The everlasting Father, The Prince of Peace.

New Testament: Luke 2:11. For unto you is born this day in the city of David a Saviour, which is Christ the Lord (Deuteronomy 6:4, John 1:14, I Corinthians 10:4).

Old Testament: Isaiah 43:10-11. Ye are my witnesses, saith the Lord, and my servant whom I have chosen: that ye may know and believe me, and understand that I am he: before me there was no God formed, neither shall there be after me. Verse 11. I, even I, am the Lord; and beside me there is no saviour.

New Testament: John 8:23-24. And he said unto them, Ye are from beneath; I am from above: ye are of this world; I am not of this world. Verse 24. I said therefore unto you, that ye shall die in your sins: for if ye believe not that I am he, ye shall die in your sins".

Old Testament: Isaiah 9:6. For unto us a child is born, unto us a son is given: and the government shall be upon his shoulder: and his name shall be called Wonderful, Counsellor, The mighty God, The everlasting Father, The Prince of Peace.

New Testament: John 14:6-9. Verse 6: Jesus saith unto him, I am the way, the truth, and the life: no man cometh unto the Father, but by me. If ye had known me ye would have known my Father also: and from henceforth ye know him, and have seen him. He that has seen me has seen the Father; and how sayest thou then, Shew us the Father?

Old Testament: II Samuel 22:32 For who is God, save the LORD? and who is a rock, save our God?

New Testament: I Corinthians 10:4 And did all drink the same spiritual drink: for they drank of that spiritual Rock that followed them: and that Rock was Christ.

In these scriptures we find Christ (Yeshua) was in his Spiritual form as God the Father, and then revealed another manifestation of Himself to become the Son of God in the flesh. It's very simple, the Spirit is the Father of the Flesh (Luke 1:30-35). Thus, when Jesus Christ says, my Father, he is speaking of his own Spirit. As an example, Jesus Christ, as a man prays to his Spirit the same way a man should pray to God.

God came down from heaven and made himself a body through the virgin Mary. God put himself (his Seed) in a woman and flesh grew around the Spirit of God (Seed). Thus, the Spirit (Seed) is the Father of the Flesh (Son). The Spirit in Christ is the same Spirit (God) who talked to Moses (I Corinthians 10:4, II Corinthians 5:19).

There is no question God was in Christ. Yet some of the apostles didn't recognize him as the same Father in the Old Testament until Jesus Christ revealed himself. The apostles' experience proves one could have been walking with the Lord for years and still not know him. (John 14:7-10).

The Jews have their bewilderment of misunderstanding concerning the Messiah and the Christians have their own bewilderment of misunderstanding concerning the Deity of Christ. Most Christians are still in the bewilderment of the Trinitarian Doctrine which is a doctrine of men and can't be understood. It's not monotheistic and it doesn't make sense. We must get a better understanding of the mystery of Jesus Christ. One of the ways we can prove the Personage of Jesus Christ is by using a two hand finger analysis.

"Jesus is Lord (Yeshua is Yahweh)"
(Gen. 17:1, Deut. 6:4, Isa. 9:6, 43:11, Luke 2:11,
John 1:10, 8:24, 58, Titus 2:13, Rev. 1:7-8)

CHAPTER 8

FINGER ANALYSIS PROVES GOD IS ONE PERSON

Let's be simple and say 3 and 1 can't be mixed. God is either three persons or He is one Person. Which one is true? Let me ask you a question. Suppose I ask you how many persons are in God in this manner.

Hold up three fingers (3) in your left hand, and then hold up one finger (1) in your right hand. Here is the question; is God three persons as your left hand suggests or is God one Person as your right hand suggests?

Most of people, I asked in the past, have told me if they had to choose one while looking at their fingers; they would have to say God is one Person. And they would be absolutely correct.

Now, if God is one Person like your heart just told you He is; three persons of God is false because your heart tells you it's false and it's not true. Now, based on our conclusion, let's prove by scripture God is absolutely one Person which is true and not three persons as our traditions have led us to believe (Colossians 2:8-9).

The following scriptures are scriptural proof our finger analysis is correct. God was manifested in one Person and not three persons (Colossians 1:19, 2:8-12).

Genesis 1:1, John 1:1, 10	(God is one Person–Jesus Christ (Yeshua)
Genesis 17:1, Revelation 1:7-8	(God is one Person–Jesus Christ (Yeshua)
Exodus 3:14, John 8:58	(God is one Person–Jesus Christ (Yeshua)
Exodus 29:46, Luke 2:11	(God is one Person–Jesus Christ (Yeshua)
Exodus 6:3, Revelation 1:7-8	(God is one Person–Jesus Christ (Yeshua)
Leviticus 20:24, John 20:28	(God is one Person–Jesus Christ (Yeshua)
Numbers 3:41, II Thess. 1:7-8	(God is one Person–Jesus Christ (Yeshua)
Deuteronomy 6:4, Luke 2:11	(God is in one Person–Jesus Christ (Yeshua)
Isaiah 9:6, John 14:6-9, Rev. 1:8	(God is in one Person–Jesus Christ (Yeshua)
I Corinthians 10:4, Acts 9:5	(God is in one Person–Jesus Christ (Yeshua)
Matthew 1:21-23, Rev. 1:8	(God is in one Person–Jesus Christ(Yeshua)
Matthew 3:3, Isaiah 40:3	(God is in one Person–Jesus Christ (Yeshua)
John 1:1, 3, 10, 14	(God is in one Person–Jesus Christ (Yeshua)
Isaiah 43:10, John 8:24	(God is in one Person–Jesus Christ (Yeshua)
Exodus 3:14, John 8:58	(God is in one Person–Jesus Christ (Yeshua)
John 14:6-10	(God is in one Person–Jesus Christ (Yeshua)
Isaiah 43:11, Luke 2:11	(God is in one Person–Jesus Christ (Yeshua)
II Corinthians 5:19	(God is in one Person–Jesus Christ (Yeshua)

Colossians 1:19, 2:8-12	(God is in one Person–Jesus Christ (Yeshua)
Titus 2:13	(God is in one Person–Jesus Christ (Yeshua)
Hebrews 1:3, 8	(God is in one Person–Jesus Christ (Yeshua)
Colossians 1:14-19	(God is in one Person–Jesus Christ (Yeshua)
I Timothy 3:16	(God is in one Person–Jesus Christ (Yeshua)
1 John 1:1-2	(God is in one Person–Jesus Christ (Yeshua)
1 John 5:20	(God is in one Person–Jesus Christ (Yeshua)
Jude 1:25–Isaiah 43:10-11	(God is in one Person–Jesus Christ (Yeshua)
Revelation 1:7-8	(God is in one Person–Jesus Christ (Yeshua)

There is nowhere in scripture where God portrays Himself as three persons. The Trinity is a manmade doctrine developed in 325AD, clarified in 381AD and continued to be transformed through four more councils, ending as a fully developed Church doctrine at the Council of Constantinople in 680 AD. There were a total of six councils to establish one Trinitarian Doctrine, which is not the doctrine of God; rather, the Trinitarian doctrine is an unsound doctrine of men. (Galatians 1:6-9, Colossians 2:8-12).

The doctrine of three persons in one God is not a doctrine followed by Jews, the original Oneness Apostolic Pentecostal Christians, Muslims, Unitarians, Jehovah's Witnesses, nor the modern day Oneness Apostolic Pentecostal Christians (i.e. the Apostles).

In addition, the Trinitarian Doctrine does not support the Shema, "Hear, O Israel: The LORD our God is one LORD: Most Christian faiths don't understand the Shema because it doesn't fit into a framework of a two or three person God. (Deuteronomy 6:4).

The truth is; the first Ecumenical Council of Roman Catholic Churches (325 & 381AD) have put limits on our freedom to know the true oneness of God by saying if a doctrine is not the Trinitarian Doctrine then that doctrine is heretical. This Trinitarian doctrine of three persons is a conspiracy and a satanic attack against Deuteronomy 6:4 concerning the oneness of our great God and Saviour Jesus Christ (Deuteronomy 6:4, Luke 2:11, John 10:30).

The Nicene Council agreed the Trinitarian Doctrine is true. If the Trinitarian doctrine is true, then, one would have to conclude the Apostles Doctrine (Acts 2:42), The Doctrine of Christ (II John 1:9), the Doctrine of baptisms (Hebrews 6:2) and the Doctrine of God (Titus 2:10) would have been deemed heretical and not true by this errant Ecumenical Council of Churches theology. Why? Because: The doctrine of the apostles/Christ/ baptisms and doctrine of God is not the Trinitarian doctrine.

Here is the question: Which one is right? The doctrine of the apostles'/ Christ/baptisms/the doctrine of God or the Trinitarian Doctrine?

Let me give you a clue. The apostles'/Christ/baptisms and doctrine of God is in the Bible and the Trinitarian doctrine is not. Which doctrine would you believe? And which doctrine would you teach new converts.

Historically, the apostles' doctrine in Acts 2:42 would have been deemed heretical by the Council of 325AD because it is not the Trinitarian Doctrine.

The aforementioned scriptures prove the Trinitarian Doctrine is itself heretical because it portrays God as three persons. Three persons is a doctrine of men, which wasn't taught by the apostles, and is not mentioned in scripture. The Trinitarian doctrine is a theological conspiracy against the oneness of God, Jesus Christ, and the Christian Church. (Galatians 1:6-9, Colossians 2:8-12, Hebrews 1:3, 8).

In other words, any oneness revelations we receive today and any revelation received by Paul directly from God would have been deemed heretical by these errant Catholic and Protestant Bishops. Why? Paul's oneness revelations were not according to the tenets of the Trinitarian Doctrine. Paul didn't know anything about the Trinity or the Trinitarian Doctrine because he and the apostles were dead before the Trinity was developed in 325AD. (Galatians 1:6-9).

Thus the legalization of the Trinitarian Doctrine by Constantine and the council of Bishops put a hindrance on any search for the truth of the manifestations of one God. (I Timothy 3:16).

We can now see how the search for the oneness of God was virtually shut down by the Nicaean Council (325AD). What a travesty of mankind to be labeled "heretical" because of one's search for the truth of Jesus Christ and the oneness of God.

The concept of a one Person God was and is deemed heretical by most Catholic and protestant Churches around the world. Even though, the Trinity of three persons is a paganistic/polytheistic concept of whom God is not and can't be proven, the vast majority of Christians want to continue believing in a paganistic Trinity. (II Thessalonians 2:7-8, I John 4:6).

In I Timothy 3:16, God was manifested as a man in one Person. Isn't it strange how man has always wanted a paganistic or polytheistic concept of God; regardless of what God has said about Himself and His oneness?

When we do our due diligence, we will find, in fact, the Trinitarian Doctrine is itself heretical. God never said he is three persons, the apostles didn't teach it, Jesus Christ never said it, and it's not in God's Word. Jesus Christ is the one Lord and God of heaven and earth and we should repent, be baptized in the name of Jesus Christ, the Rock upon which the church is built, and receive the gift of the Holy Ghost (Matthew 16:18-19, 28:19, Acts 2:38, 4:12, I Corinthians 10:4, Romans 6:3-4, Colossians 2:9-12, 3:17, Revelation 1:7-8).

The gospel of Jesus Christ, which was preached by Peter, Paul and the apostles, is the true gospel. The Trinity of God was never delivered to the saints. In addition, Jews who are strictly monotheistic would never think of such a strange doctrine of three persons in one God. (Galatians 1:6-9).

We might not understand it, but Jesus Christ is both God and Man and he is one Person. In this book, *"Understanding the Oneness of God,"* we will prove God is absolutely one Person in Jesus Christ. But here is the question; can Jews and Christians agree Jesus is God?

"Jesus is Lord (Yeshua is Yahweh)"
(Gen. 17:1, Deut. 6:4, Isa. 9:6, 43:11, Luke 2:11,
John 1:10, 8:24, 58, Titus 2:13, Rev. 1:7-8)

CHAPTER 9

JEWS AND CHRISTIANS
CAN AGREE JESUS IS GOD

Jews and Christians have a measure of truth and we can come together under one banner of faith because of our separate wilderness experiences. However, there must be an understanding of the Word of God as it relates to both the Old and New Testaments before we can merge our separate beliefs into the truth of the oneness of God in the face of Jesus Christ.

Christianity was started by Jews but Gentiles who were grafted in have taken this Jewish religion to a wilderness of misunderstanding and perversion, which is called the Trinitarian Doctrine. Neither the Trinity nor the Trinitarian Doctrine can be found in the Bible. Jews did not give Gentile Christians any reason to believe in three persons in one God. This Trinitarian doctrine is a man made doctrine and an assumption which was not preached by Paul nor the apostles (Galatians 1:6-9, Colossians 2:8-12).

The Trinitarian Doctrine was not created nor developed during the times and teachings of Paul and the apostles. The apostles were Jews who believed in the absolute oneness of God not three persons in one God. Paul and the apostles would have been called, historically, Modalists/Sabellianists/ Monarchianism/oneness. Shocking? Yes, extremely shocking!! But true. Why?

Will Daniels

The apostles believed God is absolutely one God and one Person who manifested Himself to mankind in three forms for salvation; the Father, the Son, and the Holy Spirit. The apostles did not believe in a three person God. God used three manifestations of himself not three persons for the salvation of mankind.

In the New Testament, we see the operation of God as He walked on earth as a man in the presence of the apostles who knew him as the Son of God. (Matthew 16:16, Mark 1:1)

We have an idea of what some Christians believed in the past but we don't have a clear understanding of what the Modalists/Sabellianist/ Monarchianism/oneness preached or wrote about the absolute oneness of God. Today, we continue to wrongly consider the Modalists to be heretics because they didn't ascribe to the doctrine of the Trinity. Most, if not all, of the Christian writings by Modalists were destroyed by Trinitarians after Constantine declared the Trinity and the Trinitarian Doctrine the official religion of his empire.

The Trinitarian Doctrine is a manmade doctrine which has caused a great falling away from the original gospel which was first delivered to the saints (II Thessalonians 2:3). The Trinitarian Doctrine cannot be found in the Old or the New Testament. It's a figment of man's imagination. One would have to ignore the oneness of God and use conjecture and assumptions to believe in the Trinity, a three person concept of who God is not. God never said He is three persons

All scriptures used to try to prove God is three, co-equal or distinct persons are assumptions and not proof God is three persons. There is no place in the Bible from Genesis to Revelation where God has spoken of himself as three distinct but co-equal persons.

This Trinitarian Doctrine is strange, vague, and can't be logically explained nor understood by any of today's professing Christians. The Trinitarian Doctrine is a conspiracy against Jesus Christ and the Christian Church. God is absolutely one God and one Person and not three persons as we have been led to believe by the god of this world (Job 13:1-11, Hebrews 1:3, Colossians 2:8-9).

48

In my book, *"Understanding the Trinity, three persons vs Three Manifestations,"* there are additional understandings of this confusing doctrine. If one would follow the scriptures explicitly, one would find Biblical truth and not conjecture or mindless double talk about three persons in the Godhead. God used three manifestations/forms of himself for the salvation of man, not three persons (I Timothy 3:16, I John 1:1-2).

According to Rabbi Ralph Messer in his book, TORAH: LAW OR GRACE? Kingdom PRINCIPLES for Kingdom LIVING, Rabbi Messer said,

> *"As far as the Jews are concerned, the God of the Tanakh (Old Testament) could not possibly be a "different" God in the time of the of the B'rit Chadasha (the New Testament). When most Jewish people view the typical Church portrayal of Jesus, they wonder if Christians believe that Jesus (as "God Incarnate") is somehow a different "Deity" than the God of Abraham, Isaac, and Jacob? This conundrum causes more than a little confusion as to the validity of Christianity and those who are followers of Jesus as the Jewish Messiah. It would be confusing because, if you absolutely believe in the Scriptural tenet of Adonai Echad ("the Lord is One"), then you MUST also believe that that Jesus IS the sole essence and Manifestation of God's image, character, and attributes! Put into essential Kingdom terminology, He represents BOTH positions of Creator/King AND Ambassador/Messiah!*

Rabbi Messer's understanding of the oneness of God is the exact same understanding of the oneness of God as understood by the *Oneness Apostolic Pentecostal Christian Churches*. The phrase "Manifestations of one God" is used by Messianic Jewish Christians and Oneness Apostolic Pentecostal Christians to prove God is absolutely one and not three persons. (Reference: I Timothy 3:16, I John 1:1-2).

Thus the Oneness Apostolic Pentecostal Christians and Oneness Apostolic Jewish Christians (a new term for a new revelation and a new reality) can agree there are three manifestations of one God as expressed in the Bible and not three modes or three persons (I Timothy 3:16, I John 1:1-2). Three modes or three persons of one God are manmade terms used to demonize true Christianity and the Oneness of God.

Modalism is a manmade term and should never be used to describe Oneness Apostolic Jewish Christians or Oneness Apostolic Pentecostal Christians. There really is a conspiracy against understanding the oneness of God, against Jesus Christ, and against the Christian Church by Trinitarian Christians who continually use demonized historical terms against modern day Oneness Apostolic Christians and Jews.

Messianic Jewish Christians (some have Trinitarian understanding of scripture), Oneness Apostolic Jewish Christians, and Oneness Apostolic Christians' understanding of the doctrine of Christ are so closely related that their understanding of the gospel would be enhanced if they had a closer relationship. (For example: holidays and feasts). Most Major Christian holidays are paganistic in nature and they are remnants from the development of the Trinitarian doctrine by Constantine and the Roman Catholic Ecumenical Council of Churches (325 and 381AD).

God can take Christians to higher heights and deeper depths in him if Christians would strive to get a better understanding of Messianic/Oneness Apostolic Jewish Christianity, their holidays and their feasts. And Messianic Christian Jews can get a better understanding of Oneness Apostolic Pentecostal Christianity and how it is relates to salvation.

By understanding Oneness Christianity, Jews will have a better understanding of the relationship between how to be born again (John 3:5, Acts 2:38), how the keys of the kingdom of heaven were used (Matthew 16:18-19), and how the great commission (Matthew 28:19) was carried out on the day of Pentecost (Acts 2:38). Messianic/Apostolic Jews will see how these scriptures are related and how the power of God's name is used in the born again experience in the New Testament (Hebrew: a change of status).

Jews and Christians can agree by putting scripture in juxtaposition. The Jews, Muslims, nor Christians, as a whole, believe Jesus Christ is the one God who said, "Hear O Israel: the Lord our God is one Lord". In my book, *"Understanding" the Trinity, Three Persons vs Three Manifestations,"* I put scriptures together to show there is only one Lord and his name is Jesus Christ (Yeshua HaMashiach).

Jesus Christ lets us know who he is and gives us an explanation of what he says on more than one occasion in the New Testament. To believers, we know him but to those who are without, they don't know him. His Words are confusing, and they don't understand what Jesus Christ is saying to the saints. (John 14:5-11). Jews and Christians are coming out of a "wilderness of Church doctrine," disobedience, and unbelief.

The thread that runs through the three major religions, Judaism, Christianity and Islam is all of these faiths have a Hebrew foundation through Abraham. Judaism, which was the first established religion and

Christianity is the result of the lineage of Isaac, while Islam is a religion from the lineage of Ishmael.

The beginning of Christianity was a result of Jewish apostles who not only set the foundation for Christianity but who also welcomed Gentile participation in this great Judeo-Christian revolution. It was the Jews or Jewish proselytes who were first referred to as Christian. In these last days God is revealing how these major religions can understand the mystery of the gospel and the identity of Jesus Christ based on their training and knowledge of who he is.

There is another thread that runs through the Jews, their heritage, Christians, their beliefs, and the Islamic understanding of scripture. All faiths in their purest forms believe there is only one God. However, the glue that brings these faiths together is their search for truth.

For the purpose of this book, let's link three faiths, Judaism, Christianity and Islam as our original foundation (People of the Book). These faiths are in a constant search for the truth of the oneness of God.

For truth to be realized, Judaism, Christianity, and Islam will have to go back to their roots to see how the truth has been hindered by our lack of knowledge and to understand there is a conspiracy against the Word of God. Our disobedience, unbelief, and lack of knowledge about the Deity of Christ have hindered the truth of the gospel.

Truth is very painful when we measure it against our own traditions, beliefs, and limited knowledge of the Deity of Jesus Christ. However, there is one thing we can be sure of. We can be sure Judaism, Christianity, and Islam want to find truth in its painful reality. Truth is the unadulterated Word of God. In our search for truth, man has devised a myriad of ways to address God. We have to ask ourselves; is there a key of the kingdom of heaven; if so, what is the key or what are the keys of the kingdom of heaven?

Note: Messianic/Oneness Apostolic Jewish Christians are terms used to describe Jews who have recognized Jesus Christ (Yeshua HaMashiach) as their Messiah, their Lord, their Saviour, and their God.

"Jesus is Lord (Yeshua is Yahweh)"
(Gen. 17:1, Deut. 6:4, Isa. 9:6, 43:11, Luke 2:11,
John 1:10, 8:24, 58, Titus 2:13, Rev. 1:7-8)

CHAPTER 10

THE KEYS OF THE KINGDOM OF HEAVEN"

There is a conspiracy against the keys of the kingdom of heaven. In Matthew 16:15-19, Jesus Christ gave Peter the Keys of the Kingdom of Heaven. The gift of the keys was an extremely important event. Why don't preachers, teachers, and evangelists teach this most important detail of the Christian message of salvation? We must ask; what were the keys, when did Peter use them, where did Peter use them, what did they open? What do the keys have to do with salvation and what did the keys have to do with the great commission?

There will be Christians who will never see the correlation between being born again, keys of the kingdom of heaven, and the great commission because of unbelief. The real question is what do the keys mean? Let's put everything in a manner wherein there would be no questions.

A. What were the keys (Torah – 613 Principles) of the kingdom of heaven? The keys of the kingdom of heaven are found in Acts 2:38.

1st key) repentance, turn away from sin and follow God.

2nd key) baptism in the name of Jesus Christ (the incarnate Torah) for the remission of sins. Jesus Christ is the Rock upon which the church is built. And the gates of hell shall not prevail against it (Psalm 18:31, Matthew 16:18-19, Acts 4:12).

3rd key) the reception of the Holy Ghost. A gift God had promised (Jeremiah 31-31:33, Hebrews 8:8-10).

B.　When and where were the keys used? The keys of the kingdom of heaven were used by Peter on the day of Pentecost (The Jews - Acts 2:38, The Samarians - Acts 8:14-17, The Gentiles - Acts 10:1, 42-48).

C.　What did the keys open? The keys of the kingdom of heaven opened the door (Jesus-Yeshua HaMashiach) to the church (John 10:9).

D.　What did the keys have to do with being born again? The keys of the kingdom of heaven, explains how to be born again by water and Spirit. (John 3:5, Matthew 28:19, Acts 2:38).

E.　What did the keys have to do with salvation? The keys of the kingdom of heaven explain how the church is built upon a rock. The baptism in the name of Jesus Christ is the rock upon which the church is built and the gates of hell shall not prevail against the Jesus name baptism. (Psalm 18:31, Matthew 16:18, Acts 4:12, I Corinthians 10:4).

The keys of the kingdom of heaven were the consummation of the great commission in Matthew 28:19. Christians should not get caught up in a satanic conspiracy to come up some other way to salvation. If your understanding of salvation does not include water and Spirit, then your understanding of salvation is in error.

Today, most Christian churches are not teaching the true gospel of Jesus Christ. If one doesn't understand what Jesus Christ, Peter, Paul, and the apostles said concerning salvation and being born again, the gospel is hid to them.

Acts 2:38 answers all of the questions concerning, the keys of the kingdom of heaven, how to be born again by water and Spirit, the Rock upon which the church is built, the first sermon to open the doors to the church, and the great commission as Jesus directed in Matthew 28:19.

The Word of God is not on trial. It's our misunderstanding of the scriptures that's on trial. We have to understand the conspiracy against God's Word concerning how to be born again.

The Conspiracy against "How to be Born Again"

All scripture points to salvation and the born again experience through the power and the resurrection of Jesus Christ. In John 3:5, Nicodemus asked Jesus what he must do to be saved. Jesus replied you must be born of the water and spirit (water-baptism in the name of Jesus Christ and the Spirit - reception of the Holy Ghost). What Nicodemus didn't recognize was; this statement was a prophetic statement that would occur in the future.

The apostle Peter brought the Words of Jesus to life in the book of Acts of the Apostles (Acts 2:38). Therefore we can understand based on the words of Peter we should repent, get baptized in Jesus name for remission of sins, which is the water and receive the gift of the Holy Ghost which is the Spirit.

Keeping this in mind, Acts 2:38 is also the answer to Luke 24:47 wherein God's name will be preached beginning in Jerusalem. (Acts 9:1-5). Now, let's get a better understanding of the born again scripture, Act 2:38, and how God's name was used beginning in Jerusalem.

Acts 2:38 is the answer to John 3:5. How to be born again in Jesus name-water and Spirit).

Acts 2:38 is the answer to Acts 19:1-5 (baptism in the name of the Lord Jesus Christ.

Acts 2:38 is the answer to Matthew 16:18-19 (the rock and the keys of the kingdom).

Acts 2:38 is the answer to Matthew 28:19 (the great commission—in the name of the Father, and of the Son, and of the Holy Ghost).

Acts 2:38 is the Rock (Name) upon which the church is built. (Psalm 18:31, Matthew 16:18-19, 28:19, Acts 4:12,

Acts 2:38 answers and verifies our understanding that baptism should be performed in the name of Jesus Christ (Colossians 3:17).

Acts 2:38 is the answer to 1 Peter 3:21, baptism saves (not the putting away of the filth of the flesh, but the answer of a good conscience toward God.)

Acts 2:38 The keys and Matthew 28:19, the great commission complement the true understanding of salvation and the born again experience.

Acts 2:38 is the answer to 1 Corinthians 1:13-15. Baptism should be performed in the name of the one who was crucified. That name is Jesus Christ (Matthew 28:19, Acts 2:38).

Acts 2:38 is the answer to Mark 16:16. He that believeth and is baptized shall be saved; but he that believeth not shall be damned.

Finally, what is the relationship between Acts 2:38 and the great commission in Matthew 28:19?

"Jesus is Lord (Yeshua is Yahweh)"
(Gen. 17:1, Deut. 6:4, Isa. 9:6, 43:11, Luke 2:11,
John 1:10, 8:24, 58, Titus 2:13, Rev. 1:7-8)

CHAPTER 11

THE GREAT COMMISSION

The conspiracy against the "great commission" as it relates to salvation is extremely significant. We will have to believe God and be obedient to God's Word in Matthew 28:19. The reason the Israelites didn't make it to the Promised Land was because they were disobedient, stiff necked and ungrateful. In addition, they didn't follow the directions of God.

For example, in Numbers 20:8, God told Moses to speak to the rock to receive water. In disobedience, Moses smote the rock. This is not what God told Moses to do. (Numbers 20:11).

In addition, God told the people to take the Promised Land. However, in disbelief, the children of Israel did not go in and take the land. Therefore because of their disobedience and unbelief, they were not allowed to go in at that time. They continued wandering in the wilderness until a whole generation had passed.

In contrast to the disobedience of Moses, let's take a look at the great commission mentioned in Matthew 28:19. Jesus told his apostles to baptize in the name of the Father, and of the Son, and of the Holy Ghost. Today's Christians don't realize they have been disobedient and have not followed the message of Jesus nor did they understand what Jesus said. Jesus said to baptize in the name (What is the name?)

Trinitarian and some subordinate doctrinal Christians don't baptize in Jesus name as Jesus specifically told them to do. The name of the Father, the name of the Son and the name of the Holy Ghost is Jesus Christ. The baptism in the <u>name</u> of the Father, Son, and Holy Spirit is revealed in Acts 2:38, 8:16, 19:5, Romans 6:3-4, Ephesians 4:5, Colossians 2:9-12, etc. We have not understood the Word of God; therefore, we are baptizing people in God's titles rather than his name. Reference the "name" in Matthew 28:19.

Therefore, God has allowed today's Christians who baptize in the titles of Jesus Christ rather than in his name to wander around in the bewilderment of the Trinitarian doctrine, which was developed by men at the council of Nicaea 325 AD. Christians, as a whole, don't know the Father nor the Son. They don't understand the Word of God nor do they understand what Jesus told them to do in Matthew 28:19. Some Christians have been blinded by their own disobedience, unbelief, and lack of knowledge.

Let me just say, we all have some lack of knowledge, we don't know everything. However, the mystery of the gospel has been revealed to us and we should share it with all of our Christian brothers.

Matthew 28:19 is a scripture that is taken out of context, used improperly, and causes disobedience to God's Word. If one doesn't know Jesus, how would they know what he is saying?

Let's look at what Jesus said; "Go ye therefore, and teach all nations, baptizing them in the name of the Father, and of the Son, and of the Holy Ghost". In this scripture one would have to understand Jesus did not say to be baptized in his titles, he said to baptize in the name. God's name is a strong tower that we should run to in order to be saved. God's name has the grace and saving power needed for salvation (Acts 4:12).

We have to understand the power of God's name to understand the importance of his name in this scripture. Notice the word name is singular. Therefore, we would have to understand the name of the Father is Jesus Christ (Isaiah 9:6, John 14:6-9). The name of the Son is Jesus Christ (Matthew 1:21) and the name of the Holy Ghost is Jesus Christ (John 14:26). God's name is Jesus Christ and Jesus Christ is the name used in baptism as revealed in Matthew 28:19 and Acts 2:38.

The only scripture in the Bible that satisfies Jesus Words in Matthew 28:19, Mark 16:16, and John 3:5, is the salvation message in Acts 2:38. "Then Peter said unto them, Repent, and be baptized every one of you in the name of Jesus Christ for the remission of sins, and ye shall receive the gift of the Holy Ghost". Therefore we have found the name of the Father and of the Son and of the Holy Ghost is Jesus Christ, One God and one name.

Colossians 2:9 also proves the name of the Father, Son and the Holy Ghost is Jesus Christ because the fullness of the Godhead is in the body of Jesus Christ. There is no other name whereby we must be saved (Acts 4:12).

Therefore if we baptize in the titles Father, Son and Holy Ghost, we have been disobedient not realizing we didn't understand what Jesus has clearly said about the importance of his name in Matthew 28:19. This scripture is misused to conceal a conspiracy against Jesus Christ and the Christian Church. There is no one, in the Bible, who has ever been baptized in God's titles; Father, Son, and Holy Ghost. It's not in there. Today Christians don't understand Jesus when he speaks because they don't know him (John 14:7). Neither do they understand the conspiracy against Jesus being the everlasting Father. (Yahweh).

Jesus Christ is the everlasting Father

There is a conspiracy against Jesus Christ being the everlasting Father. Even though we can prove Jesus is all that he said he is; we can also prove he is the Father just like he said he is. Let's take a look at some scriptures which show us there is only one Lord and Father of us all whose name is Jesus Christ, which is our family name.

Most Christians have overlooked or misunderstood scripture that proves Jesus is the Father. These scriptures prove Jesus Christ is the Father of heaven and earth. The Spirit of God which is the Father in the Old Testament has become the man Christ Jesus in the New Testament (John 1:1-14).

Again, let's prove what Jesus said in John 10:30, 33 and John 14:6-9 are true based on the scriptures (I and my Father are One meaning the same Person).

Jesus Christ (Yeshua HaMashiach)	The Father
Jesus is the everlasting Father (Isaiah 9:6)	The Father is Jesus Christ (John 14:6-9)
Jesus resurrects his body (John 2:19-21)	The Father will raise up Jesus (Acts 2:24)
Jesus will raise up believers (John 6:40)	The Father will raise the dead (Rom. 4:17)
Jesus will draw men (John 12:32)	The Father will draw men (John 6:44)
Jesus says he is the Father (John 14:6-9)	The Father is the Son (Isaiah 9:6, John 14:6-9)
Jesus answers prayer (John 14:14)	The Father answers prayer (John 16:23)
Jesus sends/comforter (John 16:7)	The Father will send comforter (John 14:26)

How can we not believe Jesus Christ (Yeshua HaMashiach) is God the Father of heaven and earth? Let's take another look at some more clear statements about Jesus Christ being God the Father which need no interpretations.

The prophets speak of Jesus Christ as the Father.	(Isaiah 9:6)
Jesus Christ tells the apostles he is the Father.	(John 14:6-9)
Jesus Christ gives us a clue he is the Father.	(John 8:19, 24, 28, 58)
Jesus Christ speaks of the Father in his body.	(John 10:38, 14:10)
Jesus Christ gives us a clue he is the Father.	(John 5:43, 8:19)
Jesus Christ as the Father created all things.	(John 1:10, Colossians 1:14-19)
Jesus Christ said I and my Father are one. (the same)	(John 10:30, 33)
Jesus Christ is the Father who became a man.	(Isa. 9:6, Matt. 1:23, John 1:14)

Most Christians understand Jesus Christ is the Son of God. However, they don't understand Jesus Christ is also God himself - the Father. Let's take a look at some comparison scriptures so we can clearly see Jesus Christ is the Father in the Old Testament and he is the Son (Word) in the New Testament – same Person in both the Old and New Testaments..

Again, let's prove what Jesus said in John 10:30 and John 14:6-9 is true based on the scriptures (I and my Father are one). The Son of God is also God the Father, let's prove it.

Jesus (the Son) is God the Father	God the Father is the Son – Jesus Christ
Jesus (the Son) the Almighty (Rev. 1:8)	God (the Father) the Almighty (Genesis 17:1)
Jesus (the Son) is God (Hebrews 1:8)	God (Father) Son and Holy Ghost (Colossians 2:8-9)
Jesus (the Son) is the Father (Isaiah 9:6)	God (the Father) is the Son (John 10:30, 33, 14:9)
Jesus (the Son) was pierced (Revelation 1:7-8)	God (the Father) was pierced (Zechariah 12:10)
Jesus (the Son) Lord of Lords (Revelations 17:14)	God (the Father) Lord of Lords (Deut. 10:17)
Jesus (the Son) is "I am" (John 8:58)	God (the Father) is the "I am" (Exodus 3:14)
Jesus (the Son) one Person is God (Hebrews 1:3)	God (the Father) one Person (Job 13:1-11)
Jesus (the Son) is God in one Person (Hebrews 1:3, 8)	God (Father) in one Person (Colossians 1:19, 2:9)
Jesus (the Son) will be born (Isaiah 9:6)	God (the Father) is born (Luke 2:11)
Jesus (the Son) will be born (Isaiah 7:14, 9:6)	God (the Father) is born (John 8:19, 14:9)
Jesus Word made the world (John 1:1-14)	God (the Father) made the world (Isaiah 44:24)

Finally, we can rest assured we have proven Jesus Christ is the Father and the Son. However, we still find Christians are consistently making antichrist statements against Jesus Christ being the one Lord God Almighty, the Father, and Creator of heaven and earth. Well meaning Christians have come to believe Jesus Christ is not the Father, Son, and Holy Ghost. Let me explain how God transformed himself from Spirit to Flesh and back to Spirit.

"Jesus is Lord (Yeshua is Yahweh)"
(Gen. 17:1, Deut. 6:4, Isa. 9:6, 43:11, Luke 2:11,
John 1:10, 8:24, 58, Titus 2:13, Rev. 1:7-8)

Chapter 12

God's Transformation from Spirit to Flesh

There is a conspiracy to confuse Christians about the three manifestations of God. The reason we can't understand the oneness of God is because some well meaning Christians are trying to convince us God is three persons. God is, in fact, three manifestations. We would do well if we could understand how God transformed himself from Spirit to Flesh and back to Spirit.

As aforementioned, we would have to think of the oneness of God as water, something we can understand. Water can be a liquid (the Father), solid ice (the Son), or steam (the Holy Ghost) – same water. This analogy is not an understanding of the Trinity; this is an understanding of the oneness of God.

What we see is the same water in three forms or manifestations. The only true understanding of the oneness of God is three manifestations of the same God (I Timothy 3:16, Revelation 1:7-8).

The water analogy proves the oneness of God, not the Trinity. The Trinity is not a sound doctrine. The Trinity is a doctrine of men and can't be proven by natural nor spiritual means (Deuteronomy 6:4, John 10:30)

The conclusion: God is absolutely one God, which is the same water (natural) and the same Spirit (Spiritual). God was and is One Person in another form; one God, three manifestations (Colossians 1:19, 2:8-9, I Timothy 3:16). Reference: My book: *"Understanding" the Trinity, Three Persons vs Three Manifestations.*

1. **"God Is a Spirit"**

Webster's definition of Spirit: The life principle in man, originally regarded as inherent in the breath or as infused by a deity; A divine animating influence of inspiration.

(John 4:23-26)
God is a Spirit: and they that worship him must worship him in spirit and truth. The true worshippers of God must have the Holy Ghost/Spirit of God. Jesus Christ is the Holy Spirit, and God is the one Spirit, therefore, Jesus Christ is God (Yeshua HaMashiach is Yahweh).

(I Kings 8:27, Jeremiah 23:24)
The heavens of heavens cannot contain God. God is omnipresent meaning he is in the whole universe.

God is in all places at the same time. Gods' Spirit stays in heaven and his Spirit was residing in the body of Jesus at the same time. There's nothing to hard for God; for God is a Spirit and he can be any place he wants to be, when he wants to be there. Therefore, God the Spirit can be in heaven and in the body of Jesus Christ at the same time. The scripture says the god of this world has blinded their mind (John 14:10-11, Colossians 1:19, 2:9).

(Romans 8:9-11)
The Spirit of God and the Spirit of Christ is the same Spirit. One God, same Spirit. The name of the Holy Ghost is Jesus Christ or as some say, I have The Spirit of Christ. Jesus Christ is the indwelling Spirit. This is the Spirit of the one God. Jesus Christ is the Spirit and God's name for this dispensation of Salvation (John 5:43).

God's name is the foundation and Rock of our salvation as mentioned by Peter in the baptismal formula. In Acts 2:38, the Rock is the baptism in the name of Jesus Christ and the gates of hell shall not prevail against it. (Psalm 18:31, Matthew 16:18-19, Ephesians 4:5). In addition to understanding how to be born again, we must understand how many spirits are there for salvation

2. How Many Spirits Are There For Salvation?

I Corinthians 12:13 tells us, "For by one Spirit are we baptized into one body, whether we be Jews or Gentiles, whether we are bond or free; and have been all made to drink into one Spirit".

This scriptures show us The Spirit of God is the Father Jesus Christ, The Spirit of Christ is the Son–Jesus Christ, and The Holy Spirit is Jesus Christ which is the same Spirit. Take a look at these scriptural explanations;

The Father is in Heaven as one Spirit.   (Jesus-Yeshua) John 10:30, 14:9)
The Spirit of Christ is same Spirit.   (Jesus-Yeshua) Philippians 1:19, I
        Peter 1:11)
The Holy Spirit the same Spirit.   (Jesus-Yeshua) Matthew 28:19,
        John 14:17, 18)

Ephesians 2:18 and Ephesians 4:4-6 tells us again, "There is one body, and one Spirit, even as ye are called in one hope of your calling; one Lord, one faith, one baptism, one God and Father of all, who is above all, and through all, and in you all. That one Spirit is the Spirit of Christ.

There is only one Spirit of God and that Spirit is called by many titles such as; the everlasting Father, the Deity of God, I am, the Holy Ghost, the Holy Spirit, the Spirit of God, the Spirit of Christ, Spirit of the Lord, and The Spirit of Jesus Christ. All these titles are correct and are used interchangeably in scripture. The Spirit has many titles but only one eternal name which is above every name and that eternal name is Jesus Christ, translated Jehovah Saviour (Isaiah 43:11, Acts 4:12, Jude 1:25).

Jesus tells us in John 3:5, "Verily, verily, I say unto thee, Except a man be born of water and of the Spirit, he cannot enter into the kingdom of God". Therefore, in order to enter the kingdom of God, you must receive the one Spirit through the name of Jesus Christ. This is the same thing Peter was saying in Acts 2:38 about the water and the Holy Ghost. We understand the names of the Spirit are interchangeable. But how can we understand Jesus Christ is the name of the Holy Spirit and is the Holy Spirit the Father?

3.   **Is The Holy Spirit The Father?**

The Holy Spirit or Deity of God is what is always referred to as the Father. Jesus Christ called the Spirit my Father on many occasions when he was demonstrating the difference between his dual nature of being God and Man at the same time. On occasion Jesus would tell his apostles he is the Father meaning the Deity is in him and his body is the express image of the Father. (John 14:6-11, Hebrews 1:3) When you read the scriptures, it's extremely important we understand whether Jesus is speaking as the Father (Deity) or as the Son (Flesh). The Spirit is the Father whose name *is* Jesus Christ (Isaiah 9:6, I Corinthians 10:4)

4.   **What Is The Name of The Holy Spirit?**

The name of the Holy Spirit is Jesus Christ. Jesus said, he would send another comforter in his name. The Spirit of God is the same as the Spirit of Christ, the Holy Spirit, or the Holy Ghost. When Christians say they have the Spirit of Christ or the Holy Ghost in them, what they are really saying is the name of the Holy Spirit is Jesus Christ who is God in his Spirit form.

Look at Isaiah 9:6. Jesus Christ is the name of the everlasting Father (Spirit) and the everlasting Father is the name of the Spirit of Christ (Holy Ghost). Therefore, the name of the Spirit is the Spirit of Christ. Jesus Christ is God's highest and most glorious name and he told us his highest name through the apostle Paul. (John 7:39, 14:6, 16-18, Acts 4:12, Acts 9:5).

Jesus told the apostles he would not leave them comfortless but *He* would come and be with them and *in* them. In John 14:16-20 Jesus said, I will come. In other words, Jesus Christ in the form of The Holy Ghost will come. Jesus did come back to earth in the form of the Holy Ghost on the day of Pentecost. In the 20th verse, Jesus lets the apostles know they would know he is the Father and He is in the apostles and the apostles are in him.

In II Corinthians 3:17, the scriptures tell us The Lord is that Spirit: and where the Spirit of the Lord is, there is liberty. But we all, with open face beholding as in a glass the glory of the Lord, are changed into the same image from glory to glory, even as by the Spirit of the Lord.

Thus the name of the Holy Spirit is Jesus Christ who came back as the comforter. Jesus Christ will send the Holy Spirit (John 16:7). In addition, Jesus Christ is the Spirit of Truth and the Spirit of Truth is the Holy Ghost. The apostles didn't understand how Jesus Christ could be the Father and would come back as the Holy Spirit. This same God performed all these things by himself with no help from any other persons or beings. (John 14:5-18, 15:26, 16:13-20).

Peter Walker said in his book, "The Jesus Way," the Essential Christian Starter Kit, pg. 49,

> *"But when we ask how (or in what way) Jesus is coming back, the answer from these verses is clear: by the Holy Spirit. When the Holy Spirit comes to them, this will be Jesus coming back to them".*

God is one God, three manifestations, and one salvation. God cannot be divided into various beings, separate spirits, or distinct persons. God is one, his nature is one and he always will be one. There is no way we can cut God up into distinct but co-equal persons. Why would we, with our limited knowledge, try to convince man God is three distinct persons? God is one Person and the Rock of our salvation.

5.   Who Is The Rock? Is The Rock God Or Jesus Christ?

Now we can understand Jesus Christ is LORD and the Rock of our Salvation. We are to be baptized into the name of the Rock-Jesus Christ. The apostle Paul got baptized calling on the name of the Lord Jesus Christ (The Rock), (Psalm 18:31, Matthew 28:19, Acts 2:38, 8:16, 9:5, 10:48, 19:1-5, 22:16, Romans 6:3-4, Ephesians 4:5 Colossians 2:9-12).

On many occasions God spoke of himself as the Rock who is perfect, true, just, and right. God explains another mystery. In II Samuel 22:32 and Psalm 18:31, there was a question asked and God gave the same meaning and wording in his answer. Only God could be speaking when he posed the same question using basically the same wording in the answer. The question is; who is God, save the Lord? And who is a Rock, save God? Jesus Christ is the Lord and the Rock (Deuteronomy 32:1-4, II Samuel 22:1-3, 32, Psalm 18:2, 30-32, Psalm 78:34-41, I Corinthians 10:4 – that Rock was Christ).

Now listen, this establishes a pattern and it lets us know God wants us to understand, "he is the Rock and his name is Jesus-Yeshua. Not only is God our Rock, he is the Holy One of Israel. God didn't use his highest, most blessed, and eternal name as he was leading the prophets, Judges, and the children of Israel.

The highest name of God, who is the Rock, which followed Moses out of Egypt, was Christ in His Spirit form. In these scriptures, God revealed to us his highest and most sacred name is Jesus Christ. And Jesus told Paul his highest and most glorious name in the book of Acts when was on the road to Damascus. Paul asked, "Who art thou, Lord?" And the Lord said, I am Jesus whom thou persecutest. Based on Jesus' answer, we should understand the mystery is in the body and name of Jesus Christ (Psalm 18:31, I Timothy 3:16, 1 Corinthians 10:4, Acts 4:12, John 1:10, Acts 9:5, Colossians 1:19, 2:9).

The whole Christian message is wrapped up in the death, burial, and resurrection of Jesus Christ and how the blood (God's blood) was applied to the souls of men by the born again experience. In other words, God's blood (Jesus-Yeshua) and his name (the Rock) are used in the born again experience by the baptism in the name of Jesus Christ and the gates of hell shall not prevail against the name, the Rock, or the baptism in the name of Jesus Christ. Jesus Christ is the name (rock) upon which the church is built (Matthew 16:19).

Since we have established Jesus Christ is God and the Messiah of the Jewish people, we can see how we should be baptized in Jesus name. (Acts 2:38, 20:28, Romans 6:3-4, Ephesians 4:5 Colossians 2:9-12, I Peter 3:21).

Jesus is Lord (Yeshua is Yahweh)"
(Gen. 17:1, Deut. 6:4, Isa. 9:6, 43:11, Luke 2:11,
John 1:10, 8:24, 58, Titus 2:13, Rev. 1:7-8)

CHAPTER 13

BAPTISM IN JESUS NAME

There is a conspiracy against the baptism in Jesus name. I have heard some people tell me it's not necessary to be baptized in the name of Jesus Christ to be saved. I was surprised to find out how far we have fallen from the original gospel message, which was once delivered to the saints.

God said my people are destroyed by the lack of knowledge. The apostle Paul said, if we or an angel from heaven, preach any other gospel let them be accursed. Why is baptism necessary? The reason baptism is necessary is because Jesus said so (Matthew 28:19, John 3:5, Mark 16:16).

In Mark 16:16, Jesus said, he that believeth and is baptized shall be saved and he that believeth not shall be damned. Why would we fight against Jesus and the Word of God which is so easy to understand? Baptism is absolutely necessary for salvation. (Reference: 1 Peter 3:21, Colossians 3:17)

The human race is constantly trying to find the truth and mystery of God's Word through our various methods and doctrine. There are so many religions and theories about baptism it would be difficult to come to the same conclusion concerning the oneness of God, the Deity of Jesus or that Jesus Christ is God himself. There is a conspiracy to reduce the importance, the identity of Jesus Christ, and the power of God's Word. Therefore, there is a conspiracy on how to be born again, which is based on baptism in God's name, Jesus Christ.

In this chapter you will plainly see how we have created our own wilderness experience because of unbelief in God's Word concerning baptism. The following statement is created by the doctrine of men concerning baptism:

Today it has been said; baptism is not essential to salvation

Where did the statement, "baptism is not essential to salvation," come from? Did this statement come from some evil force that contradicts God's Word? Baptism is a foundation of the born again experience as told to Nicodemus in John 3:5 by Jesus Christ himself. There is not one scripture in the Bible, which says baptism is not essential to salvation. The spirit of the antichrist has tainted the mind of men. Unbelievers have taken the Word of God and made it of none effect, not rightly, dividing the Word of truth.

If you want to see how men have gone astray, search the scriptures. When God says one thing, man will come up with a philosophy of their own which says; that's not what God meant and they will totally

contradict what the Lord God himself has said. The spirit of the antichrist has always contradicted the Word of God. The Word of God is extremely plain and unambiguous to a believer. However, to unbelievers the scriptures will become a challenge because they wrestle with the scriptures. The scriptures are so plain even an unlearned believer who doesn't have a theological degree couldn't make a mistake. (Psalm 56:5, II Peter 3:16).

When we see a scripture where Paul says, "confess with your mouth," we have to go back to the beginning of the verse to see who is speaking and to whom he is speaking. (Romans 10:1-9). You will find the brethren, to whom Paul was speaking, were the brethren who had already repented, been baptized in the name of the Lord Jesus Christ and have already received the gift of the Holy Spirit.

Therefore, the only thing they had to do was to confess their faith in Jesus Christ with their mouth and they would be saved. Taking one or two scriptures out of context without taking in consideration other scripture, which would bring light to what is being said, will cause one to error on the side of their own imaginations.

Jesus said, he that believeth and is baptized shall be saved, not he that confesses with his mouth shall be saved (Mark 16:16). All scripture must be taken in context or we will miss the whole meaning of the scripture. How could we not understand what Jesus said? We don't know what Jesus said because we either don't understand or we don't believe. The gospel is hid because of our disobedience and unbelief.

What about the thief on the cross, who was not baptized and went to paradise? (Luke 23:38-43). The thief on the cross lived and died under the old dispensation like Moses and the prophets; therefore, he was welcomed into paradise for righteousness sake. Blood washed baptism came after the death, burial, and resurrection. Jesus had not died and given the commission about baptism to the apostles (Matthew 28:19). And the apostle Peter had not declared the baptism in the name of Jesus Christ as directed by the Lord in the commission (Matthew 28:19, Acts 2:38).

The Bible is very specific about baptism. Baptism is absolutely necessary for salvation according to the Words of Jesus in Matthew 28:19. Who would dare change what Jesus Christ himself has ordained concerning baptism and the message of salvation? God forbid if anyone would twist the gospel to satisfy his or her own manmade doctrine.

There are so many scriptures that declare baptism is necessary for salvation. God's Word and the gospel message are being challenged by an evil spirit of the antichrist, meaning against Christ or against the Word of God. Now, let me address another damnable heresy in the world today.

The following statement shows the folly of a false doctrine of men and their lack of knowledge concerning the mystery of Christ.

People get baptized because they are saved not to be saved

This type statement is a foundation for people who want to get to heaven some other way. These people don't believe nor understand the gospel message (Mark 16:16). The statement, "people get baptized because they are saved not to be saved," cannot be proven nor does it have a foundation in God's Word. God determines when a person is saved. Today, in most

Christian churches, there is a way that seems right unto a man but the end is destruction.

Dr. David K. Bernard said in his book, "The New Birth," page 259. *"False doctrines existed from the earliest times. There is plenty of evidence in the biblical writings of Paul, Peter, John, and Jude that false doctrines abounded even in the days of the apostles and threatened to overwhelm the church".*

Paul said if you didn't get it from us, then it is accursed (Galatians 1:6-9). If we are not careful, false doctrine will deceive the very elect if it were possible. According to the Word of God, one cannot be saved without water baptism. According to John 3:5, you cannot enter the kingdom without the baptism in **water** and the **Spirit**. Therefore, the true answer to this question is; one must be baptized in water to be saved.

Peter tells us in I Peter 3:21 baptism saves, and then he explains how baptism saves. Baptism saves by giving us a good conscience toward God not by washing the body. A clear conscience helps us realize we've been washed in the blood of the Lamb by baptism. Baptism saves!! Is there a way for the Word of God to be more understandable? Why don't we believe?

The apostle Paul tells us in Romans 6:3-4; "Know ye not, that so many of us as were baptized into Jesus Christ were baptized into his death?" Verse 4. "Therefore we are buried with him by baptism into death: that like as Christ was raised up from the dead by the glory of the Father, even so we also should walk in newness of life". These verses are verification of what Jesus (Yeshua) said in Mark 16:16.

Jesus said in Mark 16:16;

1st You must believe
2nd You must be baptized
3rd You shall be saved
4th He that believeth not shall be damned

If we rightly divide the word of truth we will see the same order of instructions in Acts 2:38;

#1 Repent

#2. be baptized in Jesus name for remission of sins

#3. Receive the gift of the Holy Ghost (Acts 2:38, Colossians 3:17, I Peter 3:21).

Therefore the saying, "people get baptized because they are saved not to be saved," is in total conflict with what Jesus said in Mark 16:16 and what Peter said in Acts 2:38. What did Jesus and the apostle say about baptism?

"Jesus is Lord (Yeshua is Yahweh)"
(Gen. 17:1, Deut. 6:4, Isa. 9:6, 43:11, Luke 2:11,
John 1:10, 8:24, 58, Titus 2:13, Rev. 1:7-8)

CHAPTER 14

BAPTISM ACCORDING TO JESUS AND THE APOSTLES

Jesus said, you must first believe and be baptized to be saved. We are not saved and then baptized. We must first believe, repent, be baptized and then saved according to the Word of God. John 3:5, Mark 16:16, Acts 2:38, and I Peter 3:21 are in total agreement with belief and baptism coming before we are saved. When people say "we get baptized because we are saved not to be saved," we can see how Satan has taken God's Word and made it of none affect. Here is an interesting question. I've seen people who have received the gift of the Holy Spirit before they got baptized; does that mean they are saved without getting baptized?

According to the order in the Word of God, repentants are saved after they are baptized. God determines when a person is saved, not man. Our responsibility is to follow God's Word in the order given in scripture. What we do know is; we must be born of water and Spirit to be born again. In Mark 16:16, John 3:5, and Acts 2:38, baptism in the name of Jesus Christ is the rock upon which the church is built and the gates of hell shall not prevail against it (Matthew 16:18-19).

Paul tells us in Colossians 2:10-12, we are complete in him because we are buried with him in baptism, wherein also ye are raised with him through the faith of the operation of God. Peter and Paul have said the same thing on more than one occasion; you must be baptized into Christ to be raised with Christ. This verifies John 3:5, Acts 2:38, Romans 6:3-4, Mark 16:16, Colossians 2:8-12, 3:17, I Peter 3:21.

Jesus tells us baptism is essential to salvation in John 3:5, and Jesus tells us again in Mark 16:16 we will be damned if we don't believe we must be baptized. Peter tells us we are saved by baptism in I Peter 3:21. And Paul tells us we are buried with him by baptism so that we might be raised with him in the resurrection. (Colossians 2:12, Romans 6:3-4). Again, Paul said, "even if an angel from heaven comes preaching any other gospel, let him be accursed" (Galatians 1:6-9). All scripture verify, point to, and agree baptism in the name of Jesus Christ is absolutely necessary for salvation.

Therefore, if your words and your doctrine don't line up with the Word of God, your own tongue and your doctrine of unbelief will snare you. Who would defy the Word of the living God? Don't try to convince me of this damnable heresy that baptism is not essential for salvation.

Paul said, any doctrine other than the doctrine that was delivered to the saints is accursed. The statement, "People get baptized because they are saved, not to be saved," is misleading and God will judge it by his own Word.

How many times does the Word of God have to express the importance and necessity of baptism before men believe him? But what if some don't believe? Let God's Word be true and every man a liar. And if

this gospel is hid, it is hid to those that are lost.

Let me give you another example of how the gospel is hid (bewilderment) to unbelievers. Jesus said in Matthew 28:19 to be baptized in his name, yet there are Christians who baptize in his titles. We find in scripture, the name of the Father, the Son, and Holy Ghost is Jesus Christ in Acts 2:38. This is the only name the apostles used for baptism and is the only name we should use for baptism (Act 4:12, 10:48, 19:1-5, Colossians 3:17, I Peter 3:21). Baptism in Jesus name (God's name) is the rock upon which the church is built.

Listen, none of the apostles baptized in the titles of God; Father, Son, and Holy Ghost. Baptism in titles wasn't taught by the apostles; therefore, the baptism in titles is accursed. Why? Title baptisms do not mention the name of God. Christians, as a whole don't know God's name is Jesus Christ. And to be more specific, most Christians didn't understand what Jesus said in Matthew 28:19 because they don't know him.

The apostles can speak with authority having been with Jesus Christ and knowing exactly what Jesus said. If you said you are going to do what Jesus said, then follow the apostles because they knew what Jesus said. If you were baptized in the titles of God, you don't know what Jesus said. As aforementioned, baptism in the name of Jesus Christ is the Rock upon which the church is built (Psalm 18:31, I Corinthians 10:4, Matthew 16:18-19, Acts 2:38).

Paul was so concern someone would try to change the gospel he said the same statement twice in Galatians 1:6-10, "As we said before, so say I now again, if any man preach any other gospel unto you than ye have received, let him be accursed". We should not use the gospel to please men when they don't understand. We should always be factual, rightly dividing the Word of truth. Paul and the apostles never said baptism is not necessary. If the apostles didn't say it, why would we say it today?

God's Word is extremely plain and unforgiving. If one would follow the apostles' doctrine, you will be following the will of God (Acts 2:42). The apostles never, ever, under any circumstances baptized converts in the titles Father, Son, and Holy Ghost. Jesus said to baptize in the name. If you don't know the identity of Jesus Christ, then you won't get baptized in his name. Does that mean the Jews and Christians will be able to come together under one religious faith? (Matthew 28:19, Acts 2:38, Colossians 2:9).

We should try to teach each other but I don't believe Jews and Christians as a whole will ever come to the same conclusions until Jesus Christ returns and make a clear proclamation of truth. Only then will all faiths be able to see the error of our ways.

We all see through a glass darkly and no one person or faith has all of the answers about the glorious name of God. God has shed some light to the mystery and Deity of Jesus Christ. Let's take a look at some things we could say that could possibly bring the Judeo-Christian faiths closer together. We can come together;

1. By understanding there is one Lord (Deuteronomy 6:4, Ephesians 4:5)
2. By understanding the apostles' doctrine (Acts 2:42).
3. By understanding Jesus Christ is Lord (Deuteronomy 6:4, Luke 2:11, Acts 10:36)
4. By understanding Jesus Christ is the Almighty (Genesis 17:1, Revelation 1:7-8)
5. By understanding Jesus Christ is the Father, Son, and Holy Ghost (Colossians 2:8-9)
6. By understanding how Paul wanted us to speak the same thing (I Corinthians 1:1-10).
7. By acknowledging Jesus Christ the Messiah has come (John 1:41, John 4:25).
8. By understanding how to be born again. (Mark 16:16, John 3:5, Matthew 28:19, Acts 2:38).
9. By understanding the culmination of the gospel message of salvation (Acts 2:38).
10. By understanding the keys of the kingdom of heaven (Matthew 16:18-19, Acts 2:38).
11. By understanding Jesus Christ is the Father (Isaiah 9:6, John 14:6-9).
12. By understanding the meaning of Emmanuel – God with us (Matthew 1:23, John 1:10).
13. By understanding Jesus when He says; he is the Almighty (Rev. 1:7-8).
14. By understanding there is one Lord in the Old and New Testaments (Deuteronomy 6:4, Luke 2:11).
15. By understanding Isaiah–Jesus is the mighty God and everlasting Father (Isaiah 9:6, Rev. 1:8).
16. By understanding Jesus Christ is the first and last, the Almighty (Revelation. 22:12-13).
17. By understanding the mystery in the body of Jesus Christ (Colossians 1:19, 2:8-12).

18. By understanding all power in heaven and earth belongs to Jesus Christ (Matthew 28:18).
19. By understanding the Jesus name baptism is the Rock upon which the Church is built (Psalm 18:31, I Corinthians 10:4, Matt. 16:18, Acts 2:38).
20. By understanding the "Passover" in the New Testament (blood washed baptism) (Acts 2:38, 10:48).

If Jews, Christians, and Muslims can understand the mystery of God is in the body of Jesus Christ, then we can understand how we all can come into the same understanding that Jesus Christ is the Messiah. In order to understand Jesus Christ is the Messiah, we would have to understand how God is revealed in the New Testament..

"Jesus is Lord (Yeshua is Yahweh)"
(Gen. 17:1, Deut. 6:4, Isa. 9:6, 43:11, Luke 2:11,
John 1:10, 8:24, 58, Titus 2:13, Rev. 1:7-8)

CHAPTER 15

GOD IS REVEALED IN THE NEW TESTAMENT

The Lord God Almighty in the New Testament is the same Lord God Almighty in the Old Testament. God manifested Himself into another form (Jesus Christ) for the salvation of man. God is three manifestations of one Person–Father, Son, and Holy Ghost.

New Testament	Old Testament
Jesus created all things (Colossians 1:14-19)	God (Yahweh) created all things (Isaiah 45:18)
Jesus is the first and last (Rev.1:11)	God (Yahweh) first and the last (Isaiah 48:12)
Jesus is the Saviour (Luke 2:11)	God (Yahweh) is the Saviour (Isaiah 43:11)
Jesus is the Father (John 14:6-9)	God (Yahweh) is the Father (Isaiah 9:6)
Jesus Christ is "I am" (John 8:58)	God (Yahweh) is "I am" (Exodus 3:14)
Jesus sits on the throne (Heb. 1:8)	God (Yahweh) sits on the Throne (Psalm 45:6)
Jesus is the flesh of God (John 1:1,14)	God (Yahweh) becomes a man (Isaiah 9:6)
Jesus is the one Spirit (John 14:26)	God (Yahweh) is one Spirit (Genesis 1:1-2)

Jesus was pierced (Revelation 1:7)	God (Yahweh) was pierced (Zechariah 12:10)
Jesus is God Almighty (Revelation 1:8)	God (Yahweh) is the Almighty (Genesis 17:1)
Jesus is the Lord (Luke 2:11)	God (Yahweh) is the Lord (Isaiah 43:15)
Jesus was made flesh (John 1:1-14)	God (Yahweh) will be made flesh (Isaiah 9:6)
Jesus is the Rock (I Corinthians 10:4)	God (Yahweh) is the Rock (Psalms 31:2-3)
Prepare the way for the Lord (Matthew 3:3)	Make a way for God (Yahweh) (Isaiah 40:3)
Witnesses for Jesus Christ (Acts 10:39)	Witnesses for God (Yahweh) (Isaiah. 43:10)

The following scriptures will give us another understanding that Jesus Christ is the same God and Saviour (Spirit-Jehovah) mentioned in the Old Testament and he is now revealed, as the same Saviour, in the (Flesh as the Son) in the New Testament. Jesus Christ has a dual nature. He is fully God and fully man. One God (Spirit) is in one Man (Flesh), Jesus Christ (II Corinthians 5:19, Colossians 1:19, 2:9).

God is the Saviour in the Old Testament
(Spirit)

Isaiah 43:3   God, the Holy One of Israel is the Saviour.
Isaiah 43:11   "I, even I, am the Lord; and beside me there is no saviour"
Isaiah 45:21   "There is no God else beside me; a just God and a Saviour.
Isaiah 49:26   The Lord is Saviour and Redeemer, the mighty one of Jacob.
Hosea 13:4   There is no Saviour other than God.
Psalm 106:21   God is the Saviour.

Jesus Christ is the Saviour in the New Testament
(Flesh)

Matthew 1:21, 23.   Jesus Christ will save his people from their sins.
Luke 2:11   Jesus Christ is the Lord and Saviour.

Philippians 3:20	Jesus Christ is the Saviour we are looking for.
I Timothy 1:1	Jesus Christ is God and Saviour.
II Timothy 1:9-10	Jesus Christ was God and Saviour before the world began.
Titus 1:3	Jesus Christ is God and Saviour.
Titus 1:4	Jesus Christ is God the Father and Saviour.
Titus 2:13	Jesus Christ is our great God and Saviour.
II Peter 1:1	Jesus Christ is our God and Saviour.
II Peter 2:20	Jesus Christ is Lord and Saviour.
Jude 1:25	Jesus Christ is God and Saviour

Sometimes we wonder what the early Christian theologians at the Nicaean Council were studying. They didn't understand what God said about Himself and His oneness in the Old and New Testaments. What were they thinking? God is not the author of confusion and He is not three persons. God never told any of the prophets he is a God of three persons.

Let me give you a statement and give you another understanding. I believe God will take a people out of a people. Think of it this way. It is my opinion; God is going to give people an understanding of his plan of salvation regardless of their religious affiliations. I believe God will have one people of the same mind who will understand the plan of salvation and be saved.

There are going to be some, in my opinion, who will believe right away, follow God's Word and be saved, there will be some who will want to do more research, follow God's Word and be saved, and there will be others who would rather remain in the darkness and folly of their own traditions and be lost (II Timothy 4:3-4). In addition, there are going to be some people who might say, "I want to wait on God and see what He says".

Let me give you a way to hear from God and see what He says. Read the King James Version of the Bible and God will talk to you through his Word. If you want to hear from God, hear from him by reading his Word. The Deity of Jesus Christ has been laid out before you this day, search the scriptures for yourself.

Christians should search the Word of God and come to the Lord through repentance, baptism in the name of Jesus Christ, and receive his Holy

Spirit. Jesus Christ said, no man will come to the Father but, by me. You must have Jesus name applied to your soul before you can go to the Father which is in heaven. You must go through the water baptism in Jesus name and receive the Spirit of God (John 3:5). Those who believe and get baptized will be saved and those who don't believe will be damned (Mark 16:16). Jesus Christ also said, if you don't believe I am he, you will die in your sins (John 8:24). Why? You didn't believe Jesus Christ is the God of Abraham, Isaac, and Jacob (I Corinthians 10:4). And you didn't believe you had to be baptized in the name of Jesus Christ to wash away your sins (Acts 2:38, Colossians 3:17, I Peter 3:21).

When Jesus comes back, it is my opinion, based on the Word of God, if you have repented, been washed in the blood of Jesus Christ by baptism in Jesus name, you will receive the Holy Spirit, if you haven't received it already. After salvation you will be eligible to be caught up to be with Jesus Christ. One would have to have been washed in the blood of the Lamb by baptism and have the Spirit of God before you will be able to enter the gates of Heaven.

Remember the Passover. Those who had the blood applied on their door posts were saved. Those who didn't have the blood applied were damned. Sound familiar? God is always true to his Word. Listen, you must repent and be washed in the blood of Jesus Christ by baptism in his name to be saved (passed over). Research the book of Acts (the actions of the apostles –Acts 4:12).

As we can see, over time most Christian faiths have lost their way to salvation primarily because of a three persons in one God theology. Christians, as a whole, are not rightly dividing the Word of Truth. We have to understand whether Jesus Christ is another God (person) Jehovah made. Jesus Christ is not another God.

"Jesus is Lord (Yeshua is Yahweh)"
(Gen. 17:1, Deut. 6:4, Isa. 9:6, 43:11, Luke 2:11,
John 1:10, 8:24, 58, Titus 2:13, Rev. 1:7-8)

CHAPTER 16

JESUS CHRIST IS NOT ANOTHER GOD

The New Testament explains the mystery of one God in the scripture, "Hear, O Israel: The Lord our God is one Lord". (Deuteronomy 6:4). This scripture is satisfied in the New Testament in Luke 2:11.

Hebrew Israelites/Jews couldn't possibly believe in another God. Jews were taught to teach their children and any family member the main tenant of their faith which is the belief in the oneness of God. How does this oneness view relate to Jesus Christ? Is Jesus Christ the Messiah? Is Jesus Christ the God-Man the Jews had been looking for? Has the Messiah already come? The Jewish belief is; they are looking for God to come in the flesh and they will not believe under any circumstances he would be another God. Let's take a look at the teachings of the Lord concerning the oneness of God.

Jesus Christ tells one of the scribes the first commandment

Mark 12:28-34. Jesus says the same thing He told the Jews in the Old Testament. Hear, O Israel; The Lord Our God is one Lord. I believe God knew in his infinite wisdom man would try to make him three distinct gods or persons. God told Israel not to be deceived; he is one God. Therefore, it's almost impossible for a Jewish person to believe in the Trinity based on the Word of God as they have received it. I say almost because I believe some Jews will be deceived and will believe in a Trinity because they have denied the Shema.

God tells us there is only one Father and one God who created us all

Malachi 2:1-10. We should not argue with people who believe in more than one person in God, they are profaning the covenant of our fathers without knowledge. We've heard there is one God, so why are Christians coming up with more than one Person in God. More than one person is not what God told the Prophets or the apostles.

God is the first and last and there is no God beside himself.

Isaiah 44:6-8. Jesus Christ said in Revelation 1:7-8, 11, 22:13 he is the first and last, the Almighty. God tells people who believe in one God not be afraid because we are his witnesses. God asks; is there another God beside himself? Then he answers his own question. God says he does not know of any other God. He again tells us, there's only one true God and he will make known all of his secrets (I John 5:20).

Every True Christian knows Jesus Christ is God Almighty

Isaiah 45:2-6. We might not have known God when we first got saved, however, he will make himself known and let you know he is the Lord and there is no other God.

In the New Testament God explains he is one God and his name is Jesus Christ, the Father, who made all things (I Corinthians 8:4-7). God asks us; why is it every man doesn't know this? It reminds me of the children of Israel when God brought them out of Egypt (Revelation 1:7-8, 11, 17:14, 22:13). No matter how many signs and wonders the children of Israel saw, they still failed to please God because of their unbelief. They still wanted to make some other god. Men, it seems, always want to come up with some paganistic/polytheistic concept of God. Our minds are tainted by ignorance. We don't believe God is completely one. We still want to make God three persons

We want to create a philosophy of three persons and God warned us against it in the Torah/Tanakh, the New Testament, and the Qur'an/Koran. God said, there is no God before me and there will be no other God after me. Why can't we just believe that? If you believe God is one, you won't have a problem believing Jesus Christ is a manifestation of that one God. God is one Spirit in one body. (Luke 2:11, Colossians 1:19, 2:9, II Corinthians 5:19).

There is one Lord, one Faith, and one Baptism

Ephesians 4:4-6, 13-18. There is but one Lord, one faith (apostle's faith) and one baptism in Jesus name Verse 6 shows again there is one God who is the Father and he's in us in the form of the Holy Ghost or some might say the Spirit of Christ. Therefore, the name of the Father and the Spirit of God is Jesus Christ.

God gave us prophets, evangelists, pastors and teachers to bring us into the unity of the apostles' faith and the knowledge of the mystery of Jesus Christ so we would not be carried away by every wind of doctrine. How is it we don't understand how God reconciles man back to himself? God reconciles man back to himself (Deity) through Jesus Christ (Son) by baptism. I Timothy 2:5-6. This scripture reads "For there is one God, and one mediator between God and men, the man Christ Jesus Christ (who is both God and Man).

This scripture tells us Jesus Christ is God and he is also the mediator between God and man because he gave his body as a ransom to re-seal man's relationship back to God.

In other words, God as a man will reunite us with his own Spirit. And Jesus Christ is the mediator between flesh and Spirit. Christians, as a whole, don't understand how God can perform in this manner and still be one God. God tells us if we believe in One God, we do well the devils also believe and tremble.

The devil knows there is only one Lord God

James 2:19. Why should we try to convince some Christian followers there's more than one Person in God when even Satan doesn't believe that.

Satan doesn't believe his own lie. He doesn't believe there are three persons in one God. We should use the scriptures and common sense to prove the oneness of God, rather than trying to prove three distinct persons in one God. God said he's one and the devils believe he is one.

There is no indication God has two distinct persons he consults or agrees with. God said, if there is any other God, he doesn't know of any (Isaiah 44:8). There is no God like our God. Wherefore thou art great, O Lord God: For there is none like thee, neither is there any God beside thee, according to all we have heard with our ears.

The Prophets proclaim the Oneness of God

II Samuel 7:22. There are so many scriptures that reveal the oneness of God. God has said it, the prophets have proclaimed it, Jesus Christ said it, and God has put it in our hearts that he is the only true God and there is no other (Isaiah 44:24, Philippians 2:6, 10-12, I John 5:20).

John the Baptist proclaims the coming of the messiah, Jesus Christ, which would be God in the flesh. John said, we should prepare the way of the Lord and make straight in the desert a highway for God. What God? Jesus Christ. John and Isaiah were taught in the Jewish tradition there is only one God. Therefore, they understood the one God would manifest himself in flesh. (Isaiah 40:3-5, John 1:23, I John 5:20).

Isaiah said in Isaiah 40:5. "and the glory of the Lord shall be revealed and all flesh shall see it together; for the mouth of the Lord has spoken it". Again, Isaiah said we will see God in the flesh. Jesus Christ is the Lord that is his name. I am the Lord: that is my name: And my glory will I not give to another, neither my praise to graven images. (Isaiah 42:8).

In the New Testament, Jesus Christ didn't find it robbery to be called Lord. God said, I will not give my glory to another. This lets us know Jesus Christ must have been God because God allowed his flesh to be called "Lord," and receive his glory through the passion and resurrection of Christ. Jesus Christ was glorified as God incarnate. And we are his witnesses. (Isaiah 43:10 -11, Matthew 28:18, John 1:1,14).

Which would you believe; is Jesus Christ an impostor or is he God? I feel God knew his gospel would be perverted by a three person doctrine of the Trinity, therefore, he has made it perfectly clear he is the "I am he" in both the Old Testament and New Testaments.

God is "I am he" in the Old Testament

In Deuteronomy 32:39, God said, See now that I even I, am he.

In Isaiah 41:4, God said, "Who hath wrought and done it, calling the generations from the beginning? I the Lord, the first, and with the last; I am he".

In Isaiah 43:10, God said, "Ye are my witnesses, saith the Lord, and my servant whom I have chosen:

that ye may know and believe me, and understand that I am he: before me there was no God formed,

neither shall there be after me.

In Isaiah 43:13, God said, "Yea, before the day was I am he. Jesus Christ proves that he is the Almighty God by saying the same thing he said in the Old Testament. Jesus said, I am he in the New Testament. (John 8:24).

Jesus Christ is the same "I am he" in the New Testament

In John 8:24, Jesus Christ said, "I said therefore unto you, that ye shall die in your sins: for if ye believe not that I am he, ye shall die in your sins".

In John 8:28, Jesus Christ said, "Then said Jesus Christ unto them, When ye have lifted up the Son of man, then shall ye know that I am he,"

In John 13:19, Jesus Christ said, "Now I tell you before it come, that, when it is come to pass, ye may believe that I am he".

Today, religious organizations try to prove to the world there is more than one Person in God. God consistently warns Israel he is one God and there is no God else beside me; a just God and Saviour; there is none beside me. Look unto me, and be ye saved, all the ends of the earth; for I am God, and there is none else. I have sworn by myself, the word is gone out of my mouth in righteousness, and shall not return, That unto me every knee shall bow, every tongue shall swear. Swear what? Look at Isaiah 45:21-23 and Philippians 2:10-11. Every tongue will swear Jesus Christ is Lord (Yahweh) (Deuteronomy 6:4).

Where is the man who will tell God, there are other gods or persons beside himself? Would God Lie? Could there be another God that will come after him? Is Jesus Christ the same God or another God?

Some might say God is a Spirit, therefore, Jesus Christ couldn't be God because He was Flesh. Let's examine the meaning and get an understanding of how God can be a Spirit in heaven and how He can transform himself into a man (I Corinthians 10:4). It is very important we understand how God came down from heaven through a young girl named Mary and was born as a man. The Mystery of God is in the body of Jesus Christ.

"Jesus is Lord (Yeshua is Yahweh)"
(Gen. 17:1, Deut. 6:4, Isa. 9:6, 43:11, Luke 2:11,
John 1:10, 8:24, 58, Titus 2:13, Rev. 1:7-8)

CHAPTER 17

THE MYSTERY OF GOD IS IN THE BODY OF JESUS CHRIST

There is a conspiracy that says, Jesus Christ is not the same as God (the Word). However, I submit to you; Jesus Christ appeared in a Spiritual form in the Old Testament and He was known as Jehovah, I am, Elohim, the Word, the Almighty, the Everlasting Father, I am he, etc. God came to earth in the form of a man (Jesus-Yeshua) in the New Testament (Isaiah 9:6, Luke 2:11).

The following scriptures will give you a clear understanding of how Jesus Christ is Lord. Jesus Christ is the same God in both the Old (Spirit) and New Testament (Flesh).

Old Testament	New Testament
Genesis 1:1 (God is the Creator)	Colossians 1:13-19 (Jesus is the Creator)
Genesis 17:1 (God is the Almighty)	Revelation 1:8 (Jesus is the Almighty)
Exodus 3:14 ("I am" is God)	John 8:58 (Jesus is "I am")
Deuteronomy 6:4 (God is one Lord)	Luke 2:11 (Jesus is the one Lord)
Deuteronomy 32:4 (God is the Rock)	I Corinthians 10:4 (Jesus is the Rock)

Isaiah 43:10-12 (God is the Saviour) Matt. 1:21, 23, Lk 2:11
                                       (Jesus is the Saviour)
Isaiah 44:6 (God is the first and last) Rev. 1:17, 22:13
                                       (Jesus is the first and last)
Isaiah 45:22-23 (Every knee will   Phil. 2:10-11
bow- God)   (Every knee will bow to Jesus).

Christians can understand the oneness of God in the Old Testament, however, in the New Testament we get lost in philosophy, confusion, and tradition. In the New Testament, we make an assumption God is three persons. Where did that come from? God never spoke of Himself as three persons, neither is there a concept of a Trinity in the Bible. The Trinity of three persons is a figment of man's imagination.

The following scriptures in the next chapter will give you a clearer understanding of God. In addition, we can see how God, who is Jesus Christ, is revealed in the New Testament. People have known Jesus Christ as the Son but they don't glorify him as God; "Jehovah". (Romans 1:21). Early Christians, including Paul and the other apostles, spoke of Jesus Christ as if he were God and worshipped him as God (Matthew 28:9).

If we don't worship Jesus Christ as God, we will become fools because we are still hanging on to the traditions of heathens. (Romans 1:22). Colossians 2:8-12 clears up the mystery of the oneness of God and

lets us know there is only one Person in the Godhead and that Person is Jesus Christ and we are complete in him. The following scriptures reveal the mystery in the body of Jesus Christ.

Romans 1:19-22.   God has shown his peoples the Mystery of the
                      Godhead in Jesus.
II Corinthians 5:19   God was in Christ reconciling the world unto
                      himself.
Colossians 1:19, 2:8-12 The fullness of the Godhead is in the body of
                      Jesus Christ.
Colossians 1:13-29   Jesus Christ is the image of God and the creator
                      of all things.

| I Timothy 3:16 | God was manifested in the flesh. |
| I John.1:1-2 | God was manifested and we have seen it. (John 1:1, 14, Hebrews 1:3, 8). |

II Corinthians 4:3-6 says, this gospel is hid to them that are lost. Some Christians' minds are blinded by the god of this world and they cannot see Jesus Christ is the one and only true God. (I John 5:20). If one would remember, I Timothy 3:16, God was manifested in the flesh, we can understand Colossians 1:15 which states, "who is the image of the invisible God, the first born of every creature".

Look at this question. How could Jesus Christ be the first born of every creature when he wasn't even born yet? Jesus Christ was the Word before he became flesh (John 1:1-14). Jesus was born in the mind of God which makes him the first born. (John 1:1).

This gives us an opportunity to see how God speaks of past, present, and future events. God speaks of things as if they have already happened. Jesus Christ was already born in the mind of God, even though; he had not been born or manifested in the flesh.

Now, we can understand the scripture that says, "he was in the world and the world was made by him and the world knew him not (John 1:10).

God begot himself a body, in his mind, before the body was made flesh. This was decided before the foundation of the world. God as the Word became Flesh. The scriptures tell us Jesus Christ (God in his Spirit) created all things whether they are on earth or in heaven, visible or invisible. Jesus Christ, as the Word, created all things (John 1:10). He is also the head of the body which is the church and God will reconcile everything to himself by his own blood. (Acts 20:28, Colossians 1:12-20). Paul says he was made a minister of this same God - Jesus Christ.

Paul went on to explain; this mystery of Jesus Christ being the one and only God who made the world and everything in it, was hid from the world but is now made manifest to his saints. Colossians 1:27 shows us God would make known what are the riches of his glory and this mystery among the Gentiles; which is God in Christ who is also in you, the hope of glory.

91

Therefore, the mystery is in Jesus Christ, who is God himself, and he is in us as the Holy Spirit, and he is our hope of glory. (II Corinthians 5:19, Colossians 1:19, Hebrews 1:3, 8).

Jesus Christ is the image of God and his light, revelation, mystery, and knowledge will cause us to be saved if we would just believe. God has given us the light and the knowledge of the glory of God in the face of Jesus Christ (Colossians 3:23).

Even though some religions don't believe Jesus Christ is God, we have found most major religions want to understand the Oneness of God. Let's take a look at some agreements and/or disagreements based on major religions and the oneness of God.

"Jesus is Lord (Yeshua is Yahweh)"
(Gen. 17:1, Deut. 6:4, Isa. 9:6, 43:11, Luke 2:11,
John 1:10, 8:24, 58, Titus 2:13, Rev. 1:7-8)

CHAPTER 18

RELIGIONS AND THE ONENESS OF GOD

Judaism (Jews), Islam (Muslims), Christianity (Christians), Hinduism (Hindus), Buddhism (Buddhists), Jehovah's Witnesses (Witnesses), Seventh Day Adventist (Adventists) and the Understanding of the Oneness of God.

We can help other people understand Christianity better if we first understand their faiths and what they believe about the oneness of God.

My opinions, interpretations, translations, and conclusions are based on my own research of God's Word in the King James Version of the Bible as it relates to the oneness of God.

My purpose is to show another way of looking at the truth of God's Word so we can all, as Christians, speak the same thing about the gospel of Jesus Christ.

Paul said in I Corinthians 1:10, Now I beseech you, brethren, by the name of our Lord Jesus Christ that ye all speak the same thing, and that there be no divisions among you; but that ye be perfectly joined together in the same mind and in the same judgment. Paul states my purpose and reasonings precisely. Our search is not to condemn but to correct. Any comparison of scripture is a search for truth (II Timothy 3:16).

The following religions will be compared to Christian history, research, and the King James Version of the Holy Scriptures as they relate to the manifestations and the oneness of God and how we have all fallen into the bewilderment of Church doctrine. Let's look at some of the ways, methods, faiths, and religions men have used throughout the ages to reach God.

Judaism (Jews) and the Oneness of God

Who is a Jew? I found a reference web-site, http://en.wikipedia.org/wiki/ Hebrew morphology which shows the early, later, and modern history of Jews, divisions of Jews and the history of the Hebrew language, etc.

Let's take a look at some meanings of Jew and Judaism according to Webster's New World Dictionary, Third College Edition, pgs. 726, 730.

> *A Jew-Hebrew–yehudi, member of the tribe or kingdom of Judah: A person descended, or regarded as descended, from the ancient Hebrews of Biblical times. A person whose religion is Judaism.*

> *Judaism–The Jewish religion. A monotheistic religion based on the laws (Torah-God's teaching and instruction) and teachings of the Holy Scripture.*

In summary, a Jew is the person and Judaism is the religion. Judaism is a religion developed over time, beginning with Abraham and ending at the Messianic age. The Lord brought Abraham and his family out of Ur of the Chal'dees by his father (Te'rah). They settled in Ha'ran. In Ha'ran, God told Abram to get out of the country and leave his father's house and God himself would show him a land wherein he would dwell. God sent Abram to Canaan, a land which would be an everlasting possession. God made a covenant with Abram; not only would he give him the land of Canaan but he would also bless him to become the father of many nations.

As a result, God changed Abram's name from Abram to Abraham, a father of many nations, and he changed his wife's name from Sarai to Sarah, a mother of nations. The Children of Israel (Hebrew/Israelites/Jews) are considered God's chosen people because of the covenant made by God to Abraham and his seed.

The Children of Israel were taught the ways and oneness of God by God himself through his chosen spokesmen, Moses, Abraham, Isaac, Jacob and the prophets. They were taught in the Old Testament there's only one God. "Hear, O Israel: The Lord our God is one Lord" They were taught there is only One God and there will not be another God formed. Therefore, we can conclude the children of Israel (Hebrew/Israelites/Jews) are the original true "Oneness" people of the Bible who would have been called, historically, Modalists/Sabellianists and Monarchians, which were terms coined at the Nicene Council 325AD. (Deuteronomy 6:4, Isaiah 43:10).

According to Rabbi Messer, *"Jewish people today continue to observe the instructions of the Torah. However, this is also coupled with their belief and faith in God, NOT replaced by it. The idea that God has somehow nullified the eternal Principles of His Word is completely foreign concept to the Jewish mind. There is one and only one God. This Biblical cornerstone of the Jewish/Biblical Faith is called the Shema:*

> *"Hear O Israel! The Lord our God, the Lord is One".*
> *"Shema Yisrael! Adonai Eloheinu, Adonai Echad".*

(Deuteronomy 6:4, emphasis added)
Ibid, pg. 57

Jews can't possibly believe in the Christian doctrine of the Trinity because Christians, as a whole, would say Jesus Christ is the second person in the Trinity. This indicated to Jews in the New Testament you're talking about;

1. Jesus Christ is their Messiah   (which most didn't believe)
2. Jesus Christ is the Son of God   (which most didn't believe)
3. Jesus Christ is equal with God   (which most didn't believe)
4. Jesus Christ is a Prophet   (some believed)
5. Jesus Christ is a blasphemer   (some believed)

95

In the New Testament, some Jews could accept Jesus Christ as a prophet, a rabbi, or blasphemer, but they couldn't accept the fact Jesus Christ is equal with God, the Son of God, their Messiah, nor God himself. Neither could they accept the premise there's more than one person in the Godhead (Acts 7:37).

Therefore, Jews can't accept Christianity the way it's taught in most Trinitarian churches today. Jews can get a better understanding of the oneness of God, and the Messianic Christian message if they would follow the teachings of the Oneness Apostolic Pentecostal Christians.

If the Jews would believe in Christ as the Messiah, they would be able to see the oneness of God using the New Testament scriptures to prove the Jews are absolutely correct. There really is only one God and one Person in the Godhead and not three persons which is taught by the Trinitarian doctrine.

Orthodox Jews don't believe God's real name is Jesus Christ (Yeshua HaMashiach), the Messiah of the Jewish people. They do understand, however, that their Messiah will not be another God. They believe He will be the one and only true God, the Christ, who talked to Moses, Abraham, Isaac, Jacob, and the prophets. They understood God himself would come to earth in flesh to save his people from all worldly turmoil and political strife.

Jews, as a whole, are still waiting for their Messiah. They don't understand Jesus Christ is the Messiah they have been waiting for; even though Jesus Christ has fulfilled all the prophecies in the Old Testament (Isaiah 9:6, and Chapter 53).

Don Goldstein said in his book, "I have a Friend who's Jewish Do you?"

"Yeshua fulfilled over 300 prophecies"

It would take more faith to deceive your self that Yeshua is NOT the Messiah than to accept the FACT that He is!".

Now, let's take a look at how God has talked to Jews through his prophets to prove He is Jesus, "the Christ" (Yeshua Hamashiach).

In Isaiah 7:14, God said; Therefore the Lord himself shall give you a sign; Behold, a virgin shall conceive, and bear a son, and shall call his name Immanuel (Matthew 1:23).

In Isaiah 9:6, God said; For unto us a child is born, unto us a son is given: and the government shall be upon his shoulder: and his name shall be called Wonderful, Counsellor, The mighty God, The everlasting Father, The Prince of Peace.

Matthew 1:21, And she shall bring forth a son, and thou shalt call his name JESUS: for he shall save his people from their sins.

Verse 22. Now all this was done, that it might be fulfilled which was spoken of the Lord by the prophet, saying,

Verse 23. Behold, a virgin shall be with child, and shall bring forth a son, and they shall call his name Emmanuel, which being interpreted is, God with us (Isaiah 7:14).

Luke 2:11, For unto you is born this day in the city of David a Saviour, which is Christ the Lord. (Deuteronomy 6:4, Luke 2:11, I Corinthians 10:4).

These scriptures alone prove to the world this same God (Yahweh) in the Old Testament is the same God manifested in the flesh as Jesus Christ in the New Testament.

There are thousands of Jews who are beginning to understand the New Testament in light of their customs, traditions and the Old Testament Scriptures. Christians are looking for the day wherein all ethic divisions of Jews will return to the fold of their Messiah Jesus Christ, the God of Abraham, Isaac, and Jacob. For those who are curious, we have referenced ethnic divisions of Jews. (References: Google and Wikipedia)

Ashkenazi-Germanic Jews (Eastern Europe)
Baghdadis-Iraqi Jews (settled in India)

Bene Israel–Indian Jews (Western India)

Beta Israel–Ethiopian Jews (Falasha) African

Bukhara –(Uzbek) Jews (Central Asia) 40,000 to 50,000 live in Queens, N.Y.)

Cochin- Indian Jews (Jews in Southern India)

Gruzian–Georgian Jews (Caucasus)

Italkim–Italian Jews (Bene Roma)

Juhuro- Undo Mountain Jews or Kavkaz Jews of the eastern and northern slopes of Caucasus, mainly of Dagestan, Chechnya, Azerbaijan.

Mizrahi–Middle Eastern, North African, Asian Jews

Romaniotes–Greek Jews

Sephardi–Iberian Jews (Spanish)

Temani–Yemenite Jews of Yemen

Jews can come from any nation or any ethnic background. However, there is some Jewish literature which might not be readily available in the public library. I would suggest you read, "From Babylon to Timbuktu" by Rudolph R. Windsor, "The Two Zions," Reminiscences of Jerusalem and Ethiopia by Edward Ullendorff, "The Black Jews" by Yosef A.A. Ben-Jochannan Vol. I & II, and "Africans" Jewish Ancestry Verified," The Orlando Sentinel, Sunday, May 9, 1999, pg. A-7, New York Times. Now, let's take a look at the relationship between Christianity and the oneness of God.

"Jesus is Lord (Yeshua is Yahweh)"
(Gen. 17:1, Deut. 6:4, Isa. 9:6, 43:11, Luke 2:11,
John 1:10, 8:24, 58, Titus 2:13, Rev. 1:7-8)

CHAPTER 19

CHRISTIANITY AND THE ONENESS OF GOD

Oneness Apostolic Pentecostal Christians believe God is absolutely one God and God can manifest himself into any form he chooses for communication and salvation of mankind (John 1:10, I Timothy 3:16, I John 1:1-2).

In these last days, God has manifested himself in three major forms/ manifestations for the salvation of man; the Father, the Son, and the Holy Spirit, the embodiment of Jesus Christ.. God spoke to us through Jesus Christ who is God in his Spirit form as the Word. The Word made the world and all the things in it (John 1:1, 3, 10, 14, Colossians 1:14-19, Philippians 2:6).

Oneness Pentecostal Christians believe the gospel in the book of Acts was preached by Peter, Paul and the apostles. But the gospel has been perverted by the introduction of a more than one Person in the Godhead used by Trinitarians. The apostles who were Jews knew nothing about a Trinity and they never taught it. (Galatians 1:6-9).

Christianity (Christians) and the Trinity

Most Christians of different faiths have their foundation in a Trinitarian doctrine. The Trinity was first coined by an Old age Catholic theologian by the name of Tertullian. Look up the origin of the Trinity in the Public Library.

The understanding of the Trinity of God (three persons), is a direct contradiction to our understanding of the Shema (Deuteronomy 6:4). When one looks up the Trinitarian doctrine in the dictionary or in any encyclopedia, one will find the main concept of the Trinity is; God is three distinct persons in one God.

Trinitarians believe there is a Spiritual Person whom they call the Father; there is a natural Person whom they call the Son, and another Spiritual Person whom they call the Holy Spirit. All of these Persons both natural and Spiritual are distinct, co-eternal, and co-equal in one God.

Even though Trinitarian Christians hate to think of the Trinity as paganistic; that's exactly what it is. Thinking of God as a Trinity of three persons is basically a type of paganistic/polytheistic concept using a monotheistic theme. The Trinitarian concept does not logically fit into our understanding of the oneness of God. We have to be serious about believing in a sound doctrine (II Timothy 4:3). The Trinity is not a sound doctrine.

God gave the children of Israel a strong admonition not to be deceived by a more than one God theory. God said, "Hear O Israel, the Lord our God is one Lord". There is no room for error on this matter. The Trinitarian concept is based on the theory there is more than one Person in God. Yes, it is confusing.

Some Christians don't understand the mystery of the Godhead, they will say, no man can fully understand the Trinity. I agree no man will ever understand God as a Trinity nor will they understand his Word fully until Jesus Christ returns. However, God has given us the revelation and mystery of his oneness in the New Testament and his oneness can be proven.

When Trinitarians think of God as three persons, I wonder, do they believe there's three (3) persons in one (1) main God, which would makes 4 (3 persons plus one God) or do they believe there are two (2) persons in one (1) main God which makes 3 (2 persons plus one God), If they mean two (2) persons in one God, that is not three (3) persons in one (1) God according to the definition of the Trinity.

How this Trinitarian theory is reconciled is a mystery, very confusing. The Trinity is not a sound doctrine). (Reference: my book, *"Understanding" the Trinity, Three Persons vs Three Manifestations.* (Ephesians 4:14, I Timothy 1:10, II Timothy 4:3, Titus 1:9-16, Hebrews 13:7-9, II John 1:9)

The oneness of God can be proven. but the Trinity of God cannot be proven scripturally. The Trinity is an assumption, conjecture, philosophy, and a tradition of men. The oneness of God is truth. The Trinity of God is not true (Colossians 2:8-10).

We can prove by the aforementioned scriptures, Jesus Christ is the one Lord God Almighty and there has been a concerted effort by the antichrists, naysayers, and unbelievers who will try to prove Jesus Christ is not God the everlasting Father and the one Lord God Almighty. On the other hand, the prophets, Isaiah, John, and Jesus Christ himself says in Revelation, he is the Almighty God and the everlasting Father. (Isaiah 9:6, John 14:6-9, Revelation 1:7-8).

If anyone would try to prove Jesus Christ is not the one Lord God Almighty, they would have to discard all of the scriptures in the Bible because the Word of God talks of God himself becoming a man to save his people from their sins. (Isaiah 9:6, Matthew 1:21-23, Luke 2:11, Acts 20:28).

Let's look at just a few of the scriptures that will prove without question Jesus Christ is the one Lord God Almighty and the everlasting Father which is the Spirit in his body.

In other words, when Jesus Christ speaks of his Father, he is talking about the Spirit within Himself. The Father (Spirit) put his seed in Mary. Therefore, the Almighty God (Father-Spirit-Seed) is in Jesus not some other Lord (Deuteronomy 6:4, Luke 2:11, Colossians 2:9, John 10:30, 33, II Corinthians 5:19).

By understanding the following comparisons, we can be assured we are on solid ground, a sure foundation, and a sound doctrine. Jesus Christ said in John 10:30, I and my Father are one meaning the two manifestations of Himself are the same Person (One God). Now, let's prove what Jesus Christ said about himself is true based on scripture;

Matthew 1:23	Jesus is the same God in the Old Testament, Corinthians. 10:4
Luke 2:11	Jesus is the one Lord in the "Shema," Deuteronomy 6:4
John 1:1-14	Jesus is the God who became flesh, Isaiah 9:6
John 1:23	Jesus is the God who is coming, Isaiah 40:3
John 10:30	Jesus and God are the same, John 1:10
John 14:6-12	Jesus is the everlasting Father, Isaiah 9:6
John 8:24	Jesus is the I am he, Isaiah 43:10
John 8:58	Jesus is I am, Exodus 3:14
Ephesians 4:5	Jesus is the one Lord, Deuteronomy 6:4, Luke 2:11
John 1:10, Colossians 1:14-19	Jesus is the creator, Genesis 1:1
I Timothy 3:16	Jesus is the God who was manifested, I Corinthians 10:4
Titus 2:10, 13	Jesus is the great God & our Saviour, Isaiah 43:10-12
Jude 1:25	Jesus is God and Saviour, Isaiah 43:10-12
Revelation 1:7-8	Jesus is the Almighty, Genesis 17:1

Alister E. McGrath, wrote in his book, "Understanding the Trinity," a purely historical oneness view of God on page 121. He writes;

> *"The difficulties really begin with the recognition of the fundamental Christian insight that Jesus is God incarnate: that in the face of Jesus Christ we see none other than the living God himself".*

Dr. McGrath informs us, based on scripture, Jesus Christ is a manifestation of God himself. Modern day Oneness Christians have found what the Roman Catholic Ecumenical Council of Churches historically called Modalism/Sabellianism/Monotheism is closer to the understanding of the oneness of God in the New Testament than the Trinitarian doctrine. (I Timothy 3:16).

Jesus Christ in his Spiritual form was called the Word and that Word, which is God the Father, became Flesh. (John 1:1, 14, 14:9, I Corinthians 10:4, Acts 9:5, John 8:24, 58).

There were no other persons with God in creation. God had a whole heavenly host with him yet they did not participate in the creation. God created everything by Himself. Jesus Christ is that God, in his Spiritual form, as the Word who created the heavens and the earth (Genesis 1:26-27, Isaiah 44:24, Colossians 1:10-19).

Jesus Christ is a "manifestation" of God himself. God is definitely not a Trinity, which cannot be understood. Dr. McGrath makes it clear, God's name is Jesus Christ and we can prove it. In our effort to defend the monotheism of God, we have to prove there is a conspiracy against Jesus Christ being the everlasting Father. (Isaiah 9:6, John 14:6-9).

We can say the Trinity of God is henotheistic, tritheistic, paganistic or polytheistic, but it's certainly not monotheistic. Now, let's take a look at the relationship of Islam and the oneness of God.

"Jesus is Lord (Yeshua is Yahweh)"
(Gen. 17:1, Deut. 6:4, Isa. 9:6, 43:11, Luke 2:11,
John 1:10, 8:24, 58, Titus 2:13, Rev. 1:7-8)

CHAPTER 20

ISLAM AND THE ONENESS OF GOD

"To get a better understanding of Islam and its message, we should take a look at the meaning of Islam. The term al-islam means submission to God. The designation "Islam" comes from the Arabic root s-l-m, which relays the message of submission and peace.

Islam began when a group of followers of Muhammad was forced to leave Mecca. These Arabia members were bound together because they shared Muhammad's belief in the absolute oneness of God. And paganism is wrong in the eyes of Allah.

Muhammad is not considered the founder of Islam, he is considered, by his followers, to be a religious reformer called by God to bring all peoples back to the one true God, "Allah".

The prophet Muhammad is not worshipped as a God. He was a prophet, a man born in Mecca around 570 A.D. of earthly parents; Father-Abdullah and Mother-Amina. Muhammad's name means "highly praised". Muhammad didn't get caught up in the paganistic/polytheistic practices of his day. He abhorred pagans and idol worship. His life, his teachings, and his words, as they were received from Allah, represents a standard for devout Muslims the world over.

In the year 610, when Muhammad was about 40 years old, he was called, according to Muslims, to be a prophet. Muhammad had the practice, on occasion, of going to a cave on Mount Hira, outside of Mecca, for meditation.

One night during Ramadan, the traditional month of spiritual retreat, Night of Qadr, Muhammad was meditating and a messenger of Allah, Gabriel, appeared to Muhammad and told Muhammad to "Recite," some say Proclaim or Read. Muhammad asked a question, what shall I recite? Allah gave Muhammad instructions through Gabriel on what he needed to say. "Recite, in the name of thy Lord, who created--created man from a blood clot. Recite, for thy Lord is bountiful, who taught by the pen, taught man what he knew not".

Muhammad was afraid of what he had seen and the dramatic effect the Angel had on his life. As a result of Muhammad's encounter with Allah through Gabriel; the Qur'an/Koran was written. The miracle that makes the Qur'an/Koran believable to Muslims is the idea that Mohammed was an uneducated man who memorized the whole Quran and its teachings.

Let me be clear. Mohammed did not write the Qur'an/Koran, he memorized the entire book. Only after the death of Muhammad was there an attempt to preserve the written words of the Qur'an/Koran.

Muslims believe all peoples should follow Muhammad's teachings as an example but they should not worship him as a God. Muhammad is considered the last and the greatest prophet of the Arab world. He was the only prophet of Arab descent, a messenger God used, in their opinion, to bring all believers in the world back to the concept of the oneness of God. Muhammad's message was very simple. People should abandon paganism, abandon its' devious lifestyle, and abandon its' method of worship. Mohammed taught that all people should repent and recognize that Allah is the only true God. Therefore, the goal of the Muslims is to proclaim all peoples in the world should follow the ways of the One God (Arabic-Allah). This is the same message God gave to Abraham; God is one; but God did not call himself Allah.

The Jewish and Muslim faiths have the same basic foundation in both the Torah and the Qur'an/Koran. However, over the years they have strayed as a culture, a people, and their understanding of the scriptures. The Jews and the Arabs are, in fact, natural cousins. They are both descendants from Abraham.

God had promised Abraham he would become a great nation. However, Abraham became impatient and concerned he would not have an heir because of his age. Isn't it amazing how we all, as human, think the same way. We have a tendency to grow impatient with the promises of God.

Sarah was also concerned about Abraham not having an heir so she convinced Abraham to have a child by their handmaid, an Egyptian, by the name of Hagar. Hagar became the mother of Ishmael, the father of the Arab nation. Fourteen (14) years later, Isaac was born to Abraham and Sarah as God had promised. Isaac was born when Abraham was 100 years old and his wife Sarah was 90 years old. Isaac became the father of the Jewish nation. (Genesis 16:1-16). Isaac became the heir to Abraham because;

1. He was the first born son of Abraham and Sarah.
2. Sarah did not want Ishmael to be an heir to Abraham and God honored Sarah decision to send Hagar away.
3. God had promised Abraham he would have a son by Sarah and that son, Isaac, would be Abraham's heir. God promised his covenant would be with Isaac and all of Isaac's descendants (Genesis 16:1-16, 17:1-27).

However, God wanted Hagar to understand she would also be blessed, so God sent an angel to Hagar to inform her Ishmael would also be blessed. God promised her he would multiply her seed with a great multitude and Ishmael would have a great nation with twelve (12) princes. Thus Ishmael became the father of the Arab nations. (Genesis 16:10, 17:20).

Muslims realize all of the prophets in the Old Testament including Jesus Christ in the New Testament were Jews from the lineage of Isaac. According to Muslims, the only Arab person who is recognized as being the last prophet is Muhammad, who, according to Muslims, memorized the Qur'an/Koran as he received instructions from Allah, through Gabriel.

In summary, Jews (Judaism) and Arabic families (Muslims) were taught and trained about the oneness of God by Abraham, Isaac, Jacob, and Ishmael. Both faiths are strictly monotheistic.

Why are these three religions, Judaism (Torah/Tanakh), Christians (Old & New Testaments), and Islam (the Quran), so far apart? I found the Deity of Jesus Christ is the main issue which separates these three faiths. All three faiths in their purest forms are strictly monotheistic. However, they can't agree on the Deity nor Sonship of Jesus Christ. There is an agreement, however, among the three religions concerning a Messiah.

The Jews believe they are "the Chosen People of God". They believe Jesus Christ was only a prophet. They don't believe he was God, the Son of God, nor God's Messiah. They believe their Messiah will come and change the world sometime in the future. They are still looking for his return.

Agreement: The Messiah will come back to change the world.

The Christians believe they have been grafted in and have the same promise as the Jews. Christians believe Jesus Christ is the Messiah, "the Christ" of the Jewish people, and the Saviour of the World. Christians also believe Christ is the Son of the Living God, an epiphany/manifestation of God himself, the Almighty. We believe Jesus Christ will come back a second time as God, the Messiah, and change the world (Revelation 1:7-8).

Agreement: Jesus Christ (Messiah) will come back to change the world.

Muslims believe God, Allah, is sovereign and he has not manifested himself as a man. They do believe Jesus Christ is one of the great prophets. He is not God; neither is he the Son of God. They believe God doesn't have a Son, and they don't believe Jesus died on the cross. Muslims do believe Jesus Christ had a virgin birth and He will come again to change the world. The President of Iran wants to hasten the return of their Messiah by causing chaos and havoc in the world, which, he thinks, will cause their Messiah to return to right the wrongs of mankind.

Agreement: A Messiah (Mashiach) for Jews, the Messiah (Jesus Christ) for Christians, the Messiah (Isa al-Masih - Mahdi) for Muslims will come back to change the world.

This is the great deception: There will come a day when Islam will present a false Jesus whom the whole world will believe and be deceived. The Muslims will try to convince you that Jesus Christ is not God the Father. They will say that the real Jesus is just a prophet and not God himself. They will convince you that Allah is the one true God rather than Jesus Christ of Nazareth. Most Christians and Jews will be deceived by this anti-christ because they too don't believe Jesus Christ is God, The Father.

God has proven he is the incarnate Jesus Christ (the Father) and there was no God formed before him and neither shall there be after him. Jesus Christ (God) is I am he, the Father, and the Almighty God in both the Old and New Testaments. And if you don't believe it; you will die in your sins. You would rather believe a lie than the truth (Isaiah 9:6, 43:10, John 14:6-9, 8:24, 58).

Watch out Christians and Jews: Because of your unbelief, Islam will present a false Jesus (Mahdi) whom you will believe and be deceived. At some point, this false Jesus will proclaim Allah as God (don't believe him; he is the Antichrist). What is the antidote?

The antidote is a thorough knowledge and understanding that Jesus Christ is God himself. People who believe Jesus Christ is the one and only true God will saved and if you don't believe; you will be deceived. (Deuteronomy 6:4, Isaiah 9:6, Luke 2:11, Colossians 2:8-9, Revelation 1:7-9)

These three faiths are correct and agree, "in theory," Jesus Christ is a great prophet and will return, in the case of Jews, Christians and Muslims, a type of Messiah. Jesus Christ will reveal to us the name of the one true and Living God who spoke to our fathers Abraham, Isaac, Jacob, and Ishmael. If this Messiah says that Allah is God; he is a false Messiah.

Even though some groups might not realize it, we are all looking for the glorious appearing of the one God of heaven and earth (John 1:10, Titus 2:13, Jude 1:25, I Corinthians 10:4, Acts 9:5, Revelation 1:7-8).

Jews, Oneness Pentecostal Christians, and Muslims agree God is absolutely one God with no other persons involved and we also agree that the Trinitarian doctrine is heresy. God doesn't have any other persons in the Godhead other than himself. On the other hand, Jews and Muslims can't agree Jesus Christ (Yeshua) is the personage of God himself.

To prove the personage of God and the absolute Deity of Jesus Christ, we put like scriptures in juxtaposition so we can see the agreements in the Torah/Tanakh, the Qur'an/Koran, and the Christian New Testament. Without bias, we can agree that we "think" we are serving the same God because all three faiths say they are worshipping the God of Abraham, Isaac, and Jacob. We just can't agree on his oneness, his name, and who that one God really is.

These faiths, as a whole, don't believe God's highest name is Jesus Christ, even though; it can be proven in their own scriptures. Therefore, we can't agree that we are worshipping the same God. However, I submit to you that Jesus Christ is the God of Abraham, Isaac, Jacob, and Ishmael. God transformed/manifested himself from Spirit to Flesh and back to Spirit. (John 1:1-14, 14:17)

This chart will show Jews and Muslims they should come into the fold as Christians who believe in the absolute oneness of God. Hopefully, there will be a renewed understanding of who God is – Jesus Christ.

Title	The Jewish G-D	Islam-Allah	Jesus Christ
Yahweh, Yeshua	Yahweh, Elohim	Yahweh, Elohim	Yahweh, Yeshua
God is One Lord	Deuteronomy 6:4	Surah 45:36, 62:4	Luke 2:11, Acts 4:12
God is the Almighty	Genesis 17:1	Surah 3:18, 4:131	Revelation 1:7-8
God is the Creator	Genesis 1:1, Isaiah 42:5	Surah 7:54, 13:16	John 1:1-10, Col. 1:16
God is one God	Deut. 6:4, Isaiah 54:5	Surah 2:163, 255	Heb. 1:8, I John 5:20
God is First and Last	Isa. 41:4, 44:6, 48:12	Surah 57:3	Rev. 1:11, 22:13
God is Salvation	Psalm 27;1, Isa. 60:14	Surah 5:119, 6:16	Titus 2:13, Jude 1:25
God is Lord of Lords	Deut. 10:17, Ps 136:3	Surah 3:51, 45:36	Rev. 17:14, 19:16
God is the Saviour	Isaiah 43:11, 45:21	Surah 3:16, 6:16	Luke2:11,Titus1:4,2:13
God the forgiver/sins	Ps 130:4, Jer. 31:34	Surah 20:82, 22:60	Luke 5:20, Acts 13:38
One God one Throne	Ps 45:6, 47:8	Surah 2:255, 7:54	Heb. 1:8, Rev. 7:17

Warning: Christians, like Muslims want to evangelize the whole world with our separate faiths. The danger comes when Christians and Muslims try to put our similarities together in some way that's not pleasing to God. Christians can't compromise our faith without falling into the dangers of a satanic one world religion called in some circles; Chrislam. Very dangerous!!!

The major tenants of Christianity can't be challenged nor changed in any way in order to compromise with any other type or group of religions. The following tenants of Christianity are;

1. Jesus Christ is the one Lord and God (Deuteronomy 6:4, Luke 2:11, John 20:28)
2. Jesus Christ is the one Lord God Almighty (Isaiah 9:6, John 1:1-14, Rev. 1:7-8)
3. Jesus Christ is the everlasting Father (Isaiah 9:6, John 1:10, 14:9, 10:30, 33)
4. Jesus Christ is the Son of the living God (Matthew 16:16, 26:63, John 6:69)
5. Jesus Christ is a manifestation of the Holy Ghost. (John 14:17-20)
6. Jesus Christ died for the sins of mankind. (I Corinthians 15:3)
7. Jesus Christ is the Saviour of the world. (Isaiah 43:10-11, Luke 2:11, Titus 2:13, Jude 1:25)

8. Jesus Christ is the Father, Son, and Holy Ghost. (II Cor. 5:19, Col. 1:19, 2:8-9, I Tim. 3:16)
9. Jesus Christ is the Rock upon which the church is built (Matthew 16:18-19, 28:19)
10. Jesus Christ is the true Almighty God (Isaiah 9:6, Matt. 1: 21-23, I John 5:20, Rev.1:7-8)
11. God told us His name (Acts 9:5, I Corinthians 10:4, Revelation 1:7-8)
12. There is no other name whereby we must be saved—Jesus Christ (Acts 4:12)

Never compromise on any tenants of our Christian faith and the doctrine of our Lord and Saviour Jesus Christ, the everlasting Father of the universe (Colossians 2:8-12). Let's be clear, Christians have to understand the manifestations of the Father, Son, and Holy Ghost before they can explain the oneness of God. This brings up the concept of multiple gods and Hinduism which also preaches a Trinity of one God.

"Jesus is Lord (Yeshua is Yahweh)"
(Gen. 17:1, Deut. 6:4, Isa. 9:6, 43:11, Luke 2:11,
John 1:10, 8:24, 58, Titus 2:13, Rev. 1:7-8)

CHAPTER 21

HINDUISM AND THE ONENESS OF GOD

The Hindu religion is just as confusing and complex as the Trinitarian doctrine. Hindu beliefs are foreign to westerners and vice versa. Therefore, I will not address the concepts of statues, idols, symbols, heaven, hell nor the reincarnation of the souls of men into animals. Excusing the confusion, let's get an understanding of how the Hindu religion evolved.

The name Hindu is a mispronunciation of the name of the inhabitants who lived near the Sindhu river in India. Sindhu sounded like Hindu. Over time, Hindu evolved into being used more often and being more recognizable as the name of the people in that region. The name Hindu has a cultural and geographical significance. Today, the name Hindu is recognized by the world as the name of a religion from India. The first thing most religions would want to know is; what is the name of the Hindu God?

The Sanskrit name for the highest form of God, in the Hindu religion, is Brahma. Brahma is the invisible God who, according to the Hindus, created all things in heaven and earth. He is the one invisible and all powerful God of the Universe. The Hindus believe God can manifest himself in many forms. They believe the main forms God uses are; the Creator (Brahma), The Preserver (Vishnu), and the Destroyer (Shiva). These forms of God will go back to the primordial being (Brahma) in the end of time. Sounds like the Christian Trinity yet it is the Hindu Trinity of three gods in one, which Christians, have deemed polytheistic.

The Christian Trinity is the same as the Hindus Trinity, only the names have changed. The Hindus Trinity is Brahma, Vishnu, and Shiva. The Christian Trinity is the Father, Son, and Holy Spirit as three, distinct, co-equal, co-eternal persons. Men are drawn, for whatever reason, to a polytheistic, Trinitarian understanding of God. God warned us against it. (Deuteronomy 6:4)

Hindus believe in the beginning of each cycle of God's creation, there were wise men born who were called Maharishi, in Christianity we call them Prophets. These wise men, Maharishi, wrote, over time, four Vedas-Books/scripture–1. Rig Veda (Hymns) 2. Saam Veda (sacrificial songs) 3. Atharva Veda (scientific formulas) 4. Yajur Veda (sacrificial formulas). These books explain the wisdom and directions of God. The Vedas (knowledge and wisdom) are used, as a Bible, to give directions in both the spiritual and natural lives of men according to the word of their God. According to Hindus, God's creation and the beginning of time are recorded in the Vedas and this information has been passed down from generation to generation. These scriptural instructions were the beginning of the Hindu religion.

The Hindus believe the earth is millions of years old and during that time, there have been millions of manifestations of gods/deities. They believe God is in everything, animate and inanimate forms. For example; God is manifested in trees, animals, people, buildings, earth, wind, fire, water, sun, moon, etc.

Their belief is God can manifest himself in any form, in any place, and at any time to communicate with mankind. For example, Rama and Sri Krsna, according to the Hindus, are forms of God that were manifested and have contributed to the Hindu religion by their presence and teachings on earth for the benefit of mankind.

The following statement will be an unbelievable bombshell to most Christians. Hindus believe in many manifestations which are all manifestations of one God. Hindus might not understand the Christian faith and its operation but there are some Hindus who believe Jesus Christ could have been a manifestation of God himself. They believe God can transform

113

himself into a man and he has done so on many occasions. Because of their understanding of the manifestations of God, most Hindus wouldn't have a problem believing Jesus Christ is the one God of heaven and earth.

Believing Jesus Christ is God is the first step to salvation, according to our Christian beliefs. Christians believe; he who would come to God must first believe that he is; and he is a rewarder of those who would diligently seek him. Hindus don't diligently seek Christ because they don't understand how they must be saved through the blood of Christ. Therefore, they are not seeking salvation through the mystery and knowledge of Jesus Christ.

Is there anything in the Hindu religion that is familiar to the Christian faith? Familiar? Yes. The three (3) different, co-equal, co-eternal deities of one God (Trinity) and at least one "end time" event is similar to Christianity. According to Pandit Ramoran Hanoman, Hindus realize there is something happening in the world today that's different and tragic in terms of the events in the Middle East and the world, as a whole, but they don't all agree, the end of time or the coming of their God is near.

They do believe, however, at the end of time, their God, "Kalki," will come back and he will establish his Kingdom on earth. They believe this Person or heavenly being will be the manifestation of the one God Almighty who is also the creator of heaven and earth.

This one God will transform the world into a better place. Compare this understanding of who God is with the King James Version of the Holy Bible. "For the Lord himself shall descend from heaven with a shout, with the voice of the archangel, and with the trump of God: and the dead in Christ shall rise first:" Every knee shall bow to God, every eye shall see him, riding on a white horse (Isaiah 45:21, 22, 23, Philippians 2:9-11, I Thessalonians 4:16, Revelation 1:7, Revelation 19:11-17). Interesting!!!

In summary, do they believe in one God? They say they believe in one God who has appeared in many different manifestations and he will come back and change the world into a better place.

Now, let's go back and see the comparisons of these major religions concerning the return of a Saviour to change the world. We find;

1. The Jews are looking for their Jewish Messiah (Christians–Jesus Christ to return and change the world).
2. Christians are looking for our Messiah (Christians-Jesus Christ to return and change the world).
3. Muslims are looking for their Messiah (Mahdi) (Christians–Jesus Christ to return and change the world).
4. Hindus are looking for their Messiah (Kalki) (Christians–Jesus Christ to return and change the world).

When we address these faiths and their beliefs we can see the King James Version of the Bible is the most accurate account of the Messiah and the Deity of Jesus Christ. Christians believe Jesus Christ is the Saviour of the world and the Messiah of the world.

When we look at all of these theologies and doctrine and take all of these scriptures in context, we will see who is the one and only true God. Our Lord and Saviour Jesus Christ is the one and only true God (Isaiah 9:6, Luke 2:11, I John 5:20, Titus 2:13, Jude 1:25).

These major religions are looking for a representative of their God who will change the world. On that day we will finally see the invisible God who made himself visible by the incarnation of Jesus Christ through his virgin birth (Matthew 1:21-23).

In the scriptures God lets us know he will return in the form of Jesus Christ and change the world. God will show his true nature to all of these various religions and to the world that He (Jesus) is the one and only true God of heaven and earth (Titus 1:4, 2:13, Jude 1:25, Revelation 1:7-8).

Again, according to the King James Version of the Bible, "Every knee will bow and every tongue will confess Jesus Christ is Lord. There are some faiths which might not totally agree with the King James Version of the Bible, therefore, we have to address the beliefs of the Jehovah's Witnesses and their understanding of the oneness of God.

"Jesus is Lord (Yeshua is Yahweh)"
(Gen. 17:1, Deut. 6:4, Isa. 9:6, 43:11, Luke 2:11,
John 1:10, 8:24, 58, Titus 2:13, Rev. 1:7-8)

Chapter 22

Jehovah's Witness and the Oneness of God

The Jehovah's witnesses are an enigma in Christianity. Charles Taze Russell (1852-1916) is considered to be the founder of the Jehovah's Witnesses. In July 1879, Pastor Russell published, The Zion's Watchtower and Herald of Christ's Presence, a magazine to expound his beliefs and concepts about the meanings of the Bible as it relates to his apocalyptic vision. In 1881, the Zion Watch Tower Tract Society was formed to help spread Russell's form of evangelism to the world. Later the Zion's Watch Tower Tract Society's name was changed to the Watch Tower Bible and Tract Society. In 1931, the Society of Believers changed their name to Jehovah's Witnesses.

During World War II, Jehovah's Witnesses would not participate in the war. They refused blood transfusions, they did not celebrate holidays nor would they salute the flag of any nation, including the United States' flag.

Therefore, they were ostracized and in some cases put in Nazi concentration camps because of their practices, beliefs, and religion. The Jehovah's Witnesses' predicament reminds us of the persecution of the Jews. The Jews were ostracized because of who they were and the practice of their faith. This is not to say the Jews and the Witnesses agree in their fundamental understanding of scripture. This is just a social characterization which has similar persecutions based on their separate beliefs.

I do believe this organization has the correct focus about the name of the One God and the belief the Trinitarian doctrine is based on a paganistic/polytheistic concept of Christianity.

However, the Witnesses try to prove by the scriptures Jesus Christ is a lessor god and not The God Jehovah. (Reference: Tract, Jehovah's Witnesses, Who Are They? What do they believe, © 2000, page 13). The assertion God is a big Almighty God and a lessor god is totally incorrect. The Jehovah Witnesses' assertion of a big God and lessor god violates their belief in Isaiah 43:10-12.

The Jehovah's Witnesses translations and contradictions are in their own New World Translation of the Holy Scriptures. Look at John 1:1 which states the Word was a god". The translation in their scriptures has an indication there was another god formed. The Torah (Tanakh), the Christian Bible (Old and New Testaments), and the Qur'an/Koran tell us; there is no other God but God.

Based on Isaiah 43:10-12; Jesus Christ is either God or not a God at all. He is either Saviour or no Saviour. He certainly is not a lessor god.

Jesus Christ is the God of the Jehovah's Witnesses based on their own foundational scriptures. If this organization knows Jehovah, then they should have known Jesus Christ (John 14:7-9, Isaiah 9:6, John 8:24, John 12:44-45, Acts 4:12, Revelation 1:7-8).).

Let me say I believe the Jehovah's Witnesses have some brilliant minds in terms of trying to prove who God is; however, they have gone astray in their study of God's Word as it is written by inspired writers. But let me tell you some things I admire about the Witnesses. I think they are one of the greatest evangelical organizations in the world at spreading their understanding of God's Word door to door.

One would be hard pressed to find anyone in the United States who have not heard about the Jehovah's Witnesses. And if any country would allow them in, given time, the whole country would have heard something about the Jehovah's Witnesses.

There is another thing I have found which is admirable about the Jehovah's Witnesses. I believe they want to get as close to the original translations of God's Word as possible. However they don't realize The King James Version of the Holy Scriptures is inspired and closer to the original Hebrew and Greek writings than their New World Translation of the Holy Scriptures.

They search their scriptures trying to prove Jehovah is the Almighty, not realizing the "King James Version has a clearer focus of what they are trying to prove. All translations are versions whether we call it a translation or version. By saying the New World Translation of the Holy Scriptures is a more accurate understanding of God Word is not valid

I certainly don't want to be judgmental nor give the impression I know everything in the scriptures. I have learned we all see through a glass darkly, meaning we don't know everything, I don't know everything, I don't see everything, and neither do I have the answer to all of the mysteries of God. However, those things I do see and the revelation I do have are printed on these pages.

Let me give you an analogy. When one sees an ink blot, which is used by some psychiatrists, everyone will not see the same thing. For example, one ink blot might have the outline of a mother holding her baby. Everyone will not be able to see it right away. They will need someone to show them how to look at it in a different way, a different angle, more lighting, or more information. More information might be necessary so you will be able to see the same thing - a mother holding her baby.

Let me give you another example. If I were looking through a peep hole in a door and I could see on the other side, I could ask you to tell me what's on the other side of the door? If you are not looking through the peep hole you won't be able to see the other side and tell me what you see until I show you. I would have to say, come here, put that down, if you had something that was misleading. Now look through the peep hole. Now tell me what do you see? Once you look through the peep hole you will be able to see clearly because I have shown you a better way of looking at the same thing I have seen.

Now let me point out some things we might consider. Let's find some points of agreement based on what I know about the Jehovah's Witnesses. We can agree;

There is only One Almighty God
There is no other God
Jehovah is the only True God
Jehovah is the Word
Jehovah is the everlasting name of God
Jehovah is the only Saviour
Jehovah is the everlasting Father

Now, look through this peep hole. First, use only the "King James Version" of the Bible. The "New World Translation of the Holy Scriptures," has some things that don't agree with what I'm going to show you. Secondly, stop trying to prove the inspired Word of God "The King James Version" is not as understandable as your translation. Try to prove the King James Version is understandable as it's written, then you will be looking through my peep hole. The New Testament is not a Trinitarian covenant as you would agree. It is a oneness-monotheistic covenant espoused by Jewish traditions and writings in the Old Testament; "Hear O Israel: the Lord our God is one Lord".

Some scriptures will need revelation by the Holy Spirit to understand the oneness of God in the New Testament. However, in most of the King James scriptures, there is no need for interpretations or revelation; just belief. I will show scriptures that are easy to understand without a need for any special interpretation. Now, having said that; I would like to point out some agreements and disagreements of God's Word based on the different translations.

There is only One Almighty God

King James Version: Revelation 1:7-8. "I am Alpha and Omega, the beginning and the ending, saith the Lord, which is, and which was, and which is to come, the Almighty".

New World Translation of the Holy Scriptures: Revelation 1:7-8. "I am Alpha and the Omega, says Jehovah God, the One who is and who was and who is coming, the Almighty".

According to Revelation 1:7-8, we can agree Jesus Christ calls himself Jehovah God-the Almighty. Read the preceding verses to get the full context and understanding of who is speaking. Jesus Christ, who is Jehovah, is speaking and he is telling us he is the Almighty God, Jehovah-Saviour.

If we say Jesus Christ is not "The" Almighty God, we are in fact calling God a Liar. In addition, saying Jesus Christ is not God, the Christ, is the spirit of the antichrist, meaning against Christ. Jesus Christ is the Almighty Jehovah. There is no other God (I John 2:18-22, 4:3, II John 1:7, Isaiah 43:10-12, 45:21, Revelation 1:7-8).

There is no other God

King James Version: Isaiah 44:6,8. "Thus saith the Lord the King of Israel, and his redeemer the Lord of hosts; I am the first, and I am the last; and beside me there is no God.

Verse 8. Fear ye not, neither be afraid: have not I told thee from that time and have declared it?

Ye are even my witnesses. Is there a God beside me? yea, there is no God; I know not any".

New World Translation of the Holy Scriptures: Isaiah 44:6, 8. "This is what Jehovah has said, the King of Israel and the Repurchaser of him, Jehovah of armies, I am the first and the last, and besides me there is no God.

Verse 8. Do not be in dread, YOU people, and do not become stupefied. Have I not from that time on caused you individually to hear and told it out? And YOU are my witnesses Does there exist a God besides me? No, there is no Rock. I have recognized none".

When you read the New World Translation of the Holy Scriptures, see how it flows. Now, look at the King James Version and see how smooth the thought flows to increase understanding and clarity.

Look at these statements:

The King James Version says there is no God.
The New World Translation of the Holy Scriptures says, there is no Rock.

The King James Version, I know not any.
The New World Translation of the Holy Scriptures says. I have recognized none.

The King James Version says, there is no God. Why would the New World Translation of the Holy Scriptures say there is no Rock? Obliviously, there is no God is more understandable than there is no Rock. In addition, If God said, I have recognized none according to the New World Translation of the Holy Scriptures; this gives an indication there could be other gods but God hasn't recognized them. In the King James Version, God said; I know not any - period.

The complexity of translations leaves room for misunderstanding of God's Word. In order to get a better understanding of God's Word, one would have to study other scriptures to understand what God is saying. On more than one occasion God will repeat the same thing in a different context.

Conclusion: There is only one God and God doesn't know of any others. That means Jesus Christ is not a lessor god because God doesn't know of any god beside himself.

Therefore, Jehovah God is the only God and he has manifested himself as the Lord Jesus Christ, Jehovah Saviour. Jehovah is the only true God and his name is translated - Jesus Christ, Saviour, and the only true God. (Titus 2:13, I John 5:20).

"Jesus is Lord (Yeshua is Yahweh)"
(Gen. 17:1, Deut. 6:4, Isa. 9:6, 43:11, Luke 2:11,
John 1:10, 8:24, 58, Titus 2:13, Rev. 1:7-8)

CHAPTER 23

JEHOVAH IS THE ONLY TRUE GOD

King James Version: I John 5:20. "And we know that the Son of God is come, and hath given us an understanding, that we may know him that is true, and we are in him that is true, even in his Son Jesus Christ. This is the true God, and eternal life".

New World Translation of the Holy Scriptures: I John 5:20. "But we know that the Son of God has come, and he has given us intellectual capacity that we may gain the knowledge of the true one. And we are in union with the true one, by means of his Son Jesus Christ. This is the true God and life everlasting".

Jehovah is the Word

King James Version: John 1:1. "In the beginning was the Word, and the Word was with God, and the Word was God".

New World Translation of the Holy Scriptures: John 1:1. "In the beginning the Word was and the Word was with God and the Word was a god.

If a translation gives an indication of more than one God, then that document is in error. Also notice the small "g" which also indicates a lessor god. The foundation and translation in this version is flawed.

Isaiah 44:6-8 makes the Jehovah's Witnesses translation of John 1:1 a distortion of the Word of God which, in my opinion, is an abomination and calls God a liar.

Conclusion: Based on these scriptures, both the King James version and the New World Translation of the Holy Scriptures recognize the name of Jesus Christ as the Word of God. Jehovah's name is the Word of God and Jehovah God is KING OF KINGS AND LORD OF LORDS.

Therefore, according to these scriptures Jesus Christ is an epiphany of Jehovah Saviour, the Almighty God. Jesus Christ is the Word, therefore, Jesus Christ is God, Jehovah-Saviour. And Jehovah is the meaning of the everlasting name of God (Isaiah 9:6).

Jehovah is the everlasting name of God

King James Version: Psalm 83:18. "That men may know that thou, whose name alone is JEHOVAH, art the most high over all the earth".

New World Translation of the Holy Scriptures: Psalm 83:18. "That people may know that you, whose name is Jehovah, You alone are the Most High over all the earth".

Conclusion: There is no question that the name of God is Jehovah, the eternal and everlasting name of God. The name of Jesus Christ is interpreted as Jehovah Saviour and he is the Most High over all the earth. Jesus Christ is the express image of the invisible Jehovah God (Hebrews 1:3, 8).

Jehovah is the only Saviour

King James Version: Isaiah 43:11. "I, even I, am the Lord; and beside me there is no Saviour".

Luke 2:11. "For unto you is born this day in the city of David a Saviour, which is Christ the Lord".

New World Translation of the Holy Scriptures: Isaiah 43:11. "I-I am Jehovah, and besides me there is no saviour". Luke 2:11. "Because there was born to you today a Saviour, who is Christ the Lord, in David's City".

Will Daniels

Conclusion: Jehovah God has told us besides him, there is no saviour. Therefore, either Jesus Christ is God, Jehovah Saviour, or Luke recorded a lie because Luke said Jesus Christ is the Lord and Saviour (Luke 2:11).

I submit to you Jesus Christ is a manifestation of our God - Saviour-Jehovah (I Timothy 3:16, John 1:10, 14). Jesus Christ's name means Jehovah is my salvation, Jehovah has become my salvation, Jehovah is the Saviour. Jesus Christ is the only Saviour, therefore Jesus Christ is the only God-Jehovah. We can again see Jehovah is the everlasting Father in the following scriptures.

Jehovah is the everlasting Father

King James Version: Isaiah 9:6. "For unto us a child is born, unto us a son is given: and the government shall be upon his shoulder: and his name shall be called Wonderful, Counsellor, The mighty God, The everlasting Father, The Prince of Peace".

New World Translation of the Holy Scriptures: Isaiah 9:6. "For there has been a child born to us, there has been a son given to us; and the princely rule will come to be upon his shoulder. And his name will be called Wonderful Counselor, Mighty God, Eternal Father, Prince of Peace".

Conclusion: Look at the missing comma between Wonderful and Counsellor in the New World Translation of the Holy Scriptures. This translation indicates one attribute of God, Wonderful Counsellor.

Now look at the King James Version. Obviously God is talking about two attributes of God. 1. He is called Wonderful and 2. He is called Counselor. The New World Translation of the Holy Scriptures lost the understanding of seeing how Wonderful God is. He is not just a Wonderful Counsellor. His name is called Wonderful and a Counsellor. Subtle changes will cause an error in understanding the majesty of God's Word.

In this scripture, Isaiah 9:6, we can see Jehovah was manifested in the flesh. In John 1:1,14, we see his name is the Lord Jesus Christ, the mighty God and everlasting Father.

In John 14:6-11, Jesus Christ (Jehovah) explained to his apostles if they have seen him, they have seen the Father. He is the true God. He is the express image and manifestation of the invisible God. Jesus Christ is Jehovah-Saviour, and he is the everlasting Father (Hebrews 1:3, 1 John 1:1-2, 5:20).

Dr. David K. Bernard in his book, "The Oneness of God," Volume 1, pages 73-75, Dr. Bernard quotes more than 30 scriptures to verify Jesus is Jehovah the One monotheistic God whom the Jehovah's witnesses are seeking.

I believe God can use the Jehovah's Witnesses to help revolutionize and evangelize the world because of their commitment to his name and the glory of his being. However, this organization will have to understand the manifestation of Jehovah God based on I Timothy 3:16 and John 1:10, 14. When God shows the light of his Word and we ignore it, we will fall under our own folly because we won't recognize God as Jesus Christ, which proves we don't know him.

In Muncia L. Walls' book, "That I May Know Him," Light Ministries, P.O. Box 190, Medora, Ind. 47260, he writes an understanding on page 67-68, Jehovah God is Jesus Christ who was pierced on the cross.

Based on scripture, Jesus Christ is Jehovah God who was pierced. Trying to prove Jesus Christ is a lesser god and not "Christ," the Almighty Jehovah, is a spiritual danger that will cause us, in my opinion, based on the Word of God, to fall into the utter darkness of reprobation.

A revolutionary change in this organization will take prayer and strong organizational leadership, who will stand up for the name of Jesus Christ (Jehovah-Saviour), and a new revolutionary training program to change this organization into a dynamic force that will help carry the mystery of the gospel of Jesus Christ, which is Jehovah's name for this dispensation, to the world. They are poised to be a dynamic force for the name of their God, Jehovah Saviour, Jesus Christ (Yeshua HaMashiach).

Most Trinitarian Christian organizations, which the Jehovah's Witnesses are not, want to see themselves as monotheistic because God makes it one of the foundations of his Word and the gospel. However, we know based on their teachings, the Jehovah's Witnesses are not strictly monotheistic because they believe in Jesus Christ as a lessor god. A lessor god is Ditheism or a subordinate god theology, which is the belief in two distinct gods, a form of polytheism (a Marcion/Arianism theology). A child of God can clearly see the error in this type doctrine. Jehovah (Jesus Christ) is a monotheistic God with no lessor god or persons associated with him (Isaiah 42:8, 43:10, 44:6, 8, 24, Revelation 1:7-8).

Christians will have to learn more about the oneness of God, who is Jehovah God. And they will have to understand the Trinitarian concept of three persons of God verses three manifestations of God. Then we can get a better understanding of how and why we have turned away from the oneness of God and the true gospel of Jesus Christ who is Jehovah the Almighty God (Revelation 1:7-8)

This falling away from the gospel of Christ was foretold by the apostle Paul (II Thessalonians 2:1-3). Once we have fallen away, it's hard to get back because of our traditional teachings of the Trinity and Jehovah's name being associated with a lessor god.

We are currently in a new age of Apostasy starting from the 4th-5th centuries, which were the developmental eras of the Trinity. We must turn back to the one true God of the Jewish nation, Jesus Christ, who is Jehovah God our Saviour. Let's pray God will reveal his highest and most glorious name to the Jehovah's Witnesses. I believe God can use this organization as a dynamic force for the gospel of Jesus Christ (Jehovah Saviour).

The Seventh Day Adventist Church is another great organization which has had a unique beginning. And they have provided some of the greatest Christian services for themselves and the world.

"Jesus is Lord (Yeshua is Yahweh)"
(Gen. 17:1, Deut. 6:4, Isa. 9:6, 43:11, Luke 2:11,
John 1:10, 8:24, 58, Titus 2:13, Rev. 1:7-8)

CHAPTER 24

SEVENTH DAY ADVENTIST AND THE ONENESS OF GOD

According to Laura L. Vance, author of "Seventh-day Adventism in Crisis," subtitled Gender and Sectarian Change in an Emerging Religion, the SDA Church was started by William Miller who was born in 1782.

In her writings, Ms. Vance mentioned William Miller who studied the scriptures in what was called in his day Biblicism. Biblicism means the Bible is to be considered wholly homogenous; any passage can be used to clarify the significance of any other irrespective of context. This is the method I used because I believe the scriptures are synergistic and all scripture can be understood only as part of a whole.

In addition to Miller's method of study, he was also open to new revelations and new understandings of scripture. He found the scriptures fascinating. His understanding of the unfolding truth of God's Word matched the understanding of Ellen G. White who also believed God's Word was ever unfolding new truths, which might not have been clear in the past. Ellen White called the unfolding truth and the new revelations of God's Word - present truth. Thus the name of their magazine, *"The Present Truth,"* published in July 1849. Ms. White believed the Adventist should be open to learning present truth within the context of their present Biblical understanding.

The early Seventh Day Adventists, who were called Millerites, didn't have a unifying doctrine after the "Advent" and the great disappointment. The Adventists concluded Christ had not failed the Adventists; on the contrary, the Adventist had failed Christ and misunderstood God's intentions. This new understanding of the doctrine of the sanctuary allowed the Millerites to reconsider their thoughts about the operations of God. According to SDA's doctrine of the sanctuary, Christ had to complete his heavenly ministry and the Sabbath had to be restored as a day of worship before the "Advent" could take place.

Therefore, with their new understanding of the sanctuary doctrine and its' relationship to the Sabbath day, the Adventists had a better understanding of the great disappointment and the shortcomings of the Millerites. It was their understanding God should be worshiped on the seventh day (Sabbath-Saturday). This understanding set the Seventh-day Adventist apart from the other factions of the Millerites who didn't have a seventh day philosophy. Thus the name changes to Seventh Day Adventists rather than the Millerites Adventists.

The driving force behind the newly reformed Seventh Day Adventists Church was Ellen G. White. Through her visions and prophecy, Ellen White pushed increasingly for evangelism and missionary work among "non-believers". She supported formal organization which was once opposed by Millerites as "Babylon". She solved and enforced organizational problems, instituted dietary laws, started hospitals and sanitariums for its members, started a publishing company, and published their first magazine, "The Present Truth". Thus, the theology and foundation of the Seventh Day Adventists Church were born. (Reference: Adventists: Doomsday sect turned to health advocacy, Orlando Sentinel, May 29, 2013).

Ellen White and her revolutionary theology redefined Christian organizations, Christian Conduct, and reinstituted the Sabbath Day as a day which was changed to Sunday by the Roman Catholic Ecumenical Council of Churches (325AD).

This great woman of God with her visions and with the help of her husband and others formulated and structured the foundation of the Seventh-day Adventist Church as we know it today.

One of the many things I admire about Ellen G. White was her openness to "present truth" and the unfolding of the mystery of God's Word. She was not so dogmatic that she wouldn't embrace new revelations and new truths that could be proven. Ms. White had a willingness to change her understanding of the Word of God based on new revelations and new present day knowledge of the scriptures. She realized God's Word was ever evolving. Based on the writings of Ms. White and her willingness to accept present truth, I would like to present some present truth based on my research.

There are some great books written by the Seventh Day Adventists. However, there are two books I would like to address. One is; *"When the United States Passes the National Sunday Law" as Predicted in the Bible,* written by the Pacific Institute, P.O. Box 33111, San Diego, Ca 92163, copyright 1996. The second book is *"Seventh Day Adventist believe....... A Biblical Exposition of 27 Fundamental Doctrines,"* which will be discussed in the next chapter.

In the first book, there are a of number of Biblical foundational scriptures which support and stress the importance of keeping the sabbath day holy and what's going to happen when the U.S. changes the Laws to introduce, The National Sunday Law.

While reading this book, I was struck by the comments concerning the Catholic Church. The writer/writers of this book abhor the Catholic Church because of the changes made at the Nicaean Council (325AD).

Keeping that in mind, I would like to give you an analogy of a sermon by evangelist Mike Easter at the Pentecostals of Apopka called, "What's your Momma name?" The title is correct without the "s" on Momma.

Evangelist Easter pointed out in Genesis 25:1-6 Abraham called all of his sons together for their inheritance. Abraham gave all he had to his son Isaac who was the son of Sarah. But to his sons by his concubines he gave them gifts and sent them away.

Evangelist Easter pointed out Sarah was the "momma" of the promised seed (Isaac). Isaac had the right momma. He pointed out the mother in Revelation 17:3-6 is Rome.

Based on my comments and my inspiration from this sermon, I found out there was a church which was born in Rome. And out of Rome, the Catholic Church birthed;

1. The belief it's O.K. to persecute other Christians. This birth came from Rome, the beginning of the Catholic Church.
2. The belief in the Trinitarian doctrine. This birth came from Rome (the Catholic Church).
3. The belief God is three distinct persons or "three personalities in God. This birth came from Rome (the Catholic Church).
4. The belief it was O.K. to change from the doctrine of Christ to the Trinitarian doctrine. This birth came from Rome (the Catholic Church).
5. The belief it's O.K. to be baptized in the titles of God-Father, Son and Holy Ghost rather than God's name, Jesus Christ. This birth came from Rome (the Catholic Church).
6. The belief you can be saved by saying "I believe in my heart Jesus Christ died for my sins. And I believe in my heart and confess with my mouth the Lord Jesus Christ; I am saved, without repentance and baptism in the name of Jesus Christ. This birth came from Rome, the beginning of the Catholic Church, Trinitarian philosophy.
7. The belief sins can be forgiven by a man through confession to a priest rather than a direct relationship with God. This birth came from Rome (the Catholic Church).

Evangelist Easter went on to point out the mother in Revelation 12: 1-5 is Jerusalem.

Based on my comments and my inspiration from this sermon, I found out there was a birth in Jerusalem (Acts 2:1-42). And out of Jerusalem was birthed;

1. The born again experience (Acts 2:38). Shows the revelation of Jesus name and the oneness of God. This birth came from the beginning of the Church at Jerusalem.
2. The born again experience (Acts 2:38). The Church was built on Jesus name (Rock). This birth came from the beginning of the Church at Jerusalem.
3. The born again experience (Acts 2:38). We are allowed by God to repent by calling on the name of Jesus Christ. This birth came from the beginning of the Church at Jerusalem.
4. The born again experience (Acts 2:38). One will receive remission of sins by baptism in water in Jesus name. This birth came from the beginning of the Church at Jerusalem.
5. The born again experience (Acts 2:38). Belief in the reception of the Holy Ghost as evidenced by speaking in other tongues. This birth came from the beginning of the Church at Jerusalem.
6. The born again experience (Acts 2:38). They shall receive the gift of the Holy Ghost. This birth came from the beginning of the Church at Jerusalem.
7. The born again experience (Acts 2:38). Acts 2:1-42 is the explanation of the full gospel and the culmination of the plan of salvation. This birth came from the beginning of the Church at Jerusalem.

Some Christian denominations follow the Trinitarian doctrine, their momma name is Rome. This doctrine was birthed in Rome by the Catholic Church.

Christians who follow the Apostles' doctrine (Acts 2:38, 42) were born in Jerusalem, because this doctrine was birthed in Jerusalem, their momma name is Jerusalem.

The question is this; what's your momma name? Where were you born? Were you born in Rome or were you born in Jerusalem? Is your momma name Rome or is your momma name Jerusalem.

The conclusion of the sermon had a direct relationship with the actions of Abraham in Genesis 25:1-6 and a possible Judgment scenario. God will bring all of his sons together for their inheritance. To the ones who were born in Rome, he will send them away. And to the ones who were born in Jerusalem, God will give them all he has. Why? They had the right momma, Jerusalem.

This whole scenario is used to show the Seventh Day Adventists follow some of the same Catholic Church doctrine. And in my opinion, they don't have the right momma, Rome. Therefore, the purpose of this scenario is to introduce them to their right momma, Jerusalem, which is the present truth.

"Jesus is Lord (Yeshua is Yahweh)"
(Gen. 17:1, Deut. 6:4, Isa. 9:6, 43:11, Luke 2:11,
John 1:10, 8:24, 58, Titus 2:13, Rev. 1:7-8)

CHAPTER 25

THE SEVENTH DAY ADVENTIST'S PRESENT TRUTH

The Seventh Day Adventists should be able to quickly see that the original gospel message of Jesus Christ which was changed in Rome to the Trinitarian doctrine by the Roman Catholic Ecumenical Council of Churches. Realizing the Seventh Day Adventists abhor the practices of the Catholic Church, I feel it would not be difficult for their scholars to see the revealed "present truth". This present truth either agrees or disagrees with the Catholic Church doctrine.

Let's take a look at how the Seventh Day Adventist and their doctrine agree with the practices and doctrine of the Catholic Church which they abhor.

The Seventh Day Adventists believes in the same concept of the Trinitarian doctrine as the Catholic Church. The doctrine of a trio of divine persons is foreign to Judaism because Jews don't speak of God as three divine deities. Jews speak of God as one. (Evangelism, p.613-617, The Desire of Ages, p. 671).

The doctrine of three persons was established by the Roman Catholic Ecumenical Council of Churches. In our minds, it seems like, God is three persons but the Bible doesn't give us a firm scriptural foundation to indicate God is three persons. God never said He is three persons. Three persons in God is a figment of man's imagination, "an assumption". This Trinitarian doctrine was birthed in and came out of Rome. The Bible speaks of God as one God and one Person (Deuteronomy 6:4, Job 13:6-11, Hebrews 1:3).

The Seventh Day Adventists believe one should be baptized in the titles of God; Father, Son, and Holy Spirit. This statement is according to the Seventh-day Adventists, Elder's Handbook, Baptism, pg. 161. The Catholic Church changed the baptism from the baptism in the name of Jesus Christ to the Trinitarian formula which is used in most protestant Churches today, which includes the Seventh Day Adventists (Reference: The Public Library).

In the second book, *"Seventh-day Adventists Believe.......A Biblical Exposition of 27 Fundamental Doctrines.*

The thing that caught my attention in the second book about the Seventh Day Adventists is their understanding that Jesus Christ is the creator and Almighty God of the universe. They are absolutely correct; Jesus Christ is the creator and Almighty God of the universe. However, when the Seventh Day Adventists include the Catholic doctrine of the three divine persons of the Trinity, the focus is lost concerning the oneness of God.

The Seventh-day Adventists admit the Old Testament does not explicitly teach God is triune; however, they will say it does allude to the plurality within the Godhead. Look for it under the subject, "The Plurality within the Godhead," page 22.

In order to understand the Bible, one's total focus must be on the oneness of God. When God said, "Hear, O Israel: The Lord our God is one Lord:," God meant every Word. There is no Trinity in God. When God says, one Lord, that one Lord is Jesus Christ (Genesis 17:1, Deuteronomy 6:4, Luke 2:11, Revelation 1:7-8).

The Seventh Day Adventists are absolutely correct in keeping the Sabbath Holy, with additional new revelations. If they would get rid of the doctrine of a three co-eternal divine persons in God which the Catholic Church developed and has tried to force feed Christians, the Seventh Day Adventists, would see God is absolutely one God.

There is no Trinitarian concept of who God is. God is one God, Jesus Christ, and he has revealed himself in three different manifestations (forms) for the salvation of man. God is neither three persons nor three personalities. God is one God with one personality used in different contexts.

Once this organization understands the oneness of God, they can, through prayer, revelation, and the power of the Holy Spirit, understand Acts 2:38, which is the culmination of the gospel, Sabbath and the Ten Commandments.

In my opinion, the Seventh Day Adventist will understand the true gospel message in Acts 2:38 better than other organizations because of their abhorrence of the Catholic Church and its doctrines, which has spread to most of the Christian world.

From my study of the original leaders of the Seventh Day Adventists, Ellen G. White was more open to change her doctrine to "present truth" which does not include the doctrine of the Catholic Church (Trinity). If this organization changed its' focus to the oneness of God and discard it's Trinitarian doctrine, they could be used to help Islamic countries get a better understanding of the gospel of Christ because they worship God on the Sabbath. What a revelation!! The Seventh Day Adventists could be used to spread the gospel of Jesus Christ to Islamic countries once they understand the oneness of God from a Christian perspective. The challenge would be trying to convince Muslims Jesus Christ is God or the Son of God.

Islamic/Muslim countries believe in the absolute oneness of God with no threeism in their understanding of God. The Seventh-day Adventists could only do this great work if they would focus on the name of the one God, Jesus Christ. They must understand the message in the Old Testament concerning the Messiah and they must have a better understanding of Matthew 28:18-19, John 3:5, and Acts 2:38. There is absolutely nothing wrong with worshipping God on Saturday (Biblical Sabbath).

I believe Islamic countries would love the idea there are Christians who believe in worshipping "one" God on Saturday. However, you must understand Judaism (Jews) and Islam (Muslims) consider the Trinity to be a paganistic/polytheistic concept of who God is. Muslims won't listen to any Christian if they believe Jesus Christ is one of three persons in the Godhead.

Most Christian organizations mentioned have some great minds in terms of finding a foundation in God's Word and holding fast to that doctrine or concept. Holding on to the Sabbath is a foundational truth that is undeniable. We should do that. However, we should rightly divide the Word of truth.

How do we keep the absolute truth of God's Word as it relates to the Sabbath and the New Covenant? Our understanding of the basic concepts of the Bible and the manifestations of God will determine whether we are in the will of God.

Finally, I would like to show what I admire about the Jehovah's Witnesses and the Seventh Day Adventist concerning God's name and God's Sabbath. As aforementioned, both organizations have some brilliant Bible scholars. However, there are some issues which should be addressed by the scholars of both these great organizations. First of all, we should all understand the importance of God's name.

"Jesus is Lord (Yeshua is Yahweh)"
(Gen. 17:1, Deut. 6:4, Isa. 9:6, 43:11, Luke 2:11,
John 1:10, 8:24, 58, Titus 2:13, Rev. 1:7-8)

CHAPTER 26

GOD'S NAME

The Jehovah's witnesses are right to hold tenaciously to God's name. The saving power of God's name is a foundational truth that is undeniable and cannot be challenged. However, they must go on to perfection by studying God's Word to get a better understanding of how Jehovah God's name was manifested, glorified, and proven to be the highest name of God, Jesus Christ (Matthew 28:18, John 1:1, 14, Acts 4:12).

By understanding God's name is Jesus Christ, in this dispensation, they can go on to understand how God's name was used for repentance and remission of sins through the blood of Jesus Christ. They would also understand the operation and reception of God's Active Force/Holy Spirit, to the lives of men (Acts 2:38). Yes, I do believe one should hold tenaciously to God's highest name. And that name is Jesus Christ which is translated - Jehovah Saviour. There is proof in Isaiah 43:10-15 and Luke 2:11. Now, let's take a look at the Seventh Day Adventists and God's Sabbath.

God's Sabbath

What I like about The Seventh Day Adventists is their revolutionary Christian understanding of education, health, and organization. The Seventh Day Adventist is one of the greatest Christian organizations at developing Christian education (Colleges/Universities) and health care facilities (Hospitals and Sanitariums). Ellen G. White, one of the greatest visionaries the world has ever seen in recent memory, created a new understanding of Christian theology which reintroduced the Sabbath Day to Christianity. I also like the idea they understand God's highest name is Jesus Christ. And they are absolutely correct in holding on to God's Sabbath.

However, they must build upon this knowledge by studying God's Word to get a better understanding of the Sabbath and how all of the Law (Torah – God's teaching and instruction) was fulfilled and incorporated into the body of Jesus Christ, for he is Lord of the sabbath (Hebrews 1:8, Matthew 12:8, Mark 2:28, Luke 6:5).

In other words, if we would seek for the knowledge and understanding of Jesus Christ, we would find he was manifested as the Holy Ghost and this transformation was and is the method God uses to apply the Law (Torah – God's teaching and instructions) and the Sabbath to our hearts. (Ezekiel 36:26-27).

In Jeremiah 31:31-33, God said he would make a new covenant and that new covenant would be put in our inward parts, and he would write the new covenant in our hearts and he would be our God and we would be his people. The new covenant was written on our hearts by God's Holy Spirit so we could keep the law (Torah – God's teaching and instructions).

In Ezekiel 36:26-27. God says he would give us a new heart and a new spirit. He would take away our stony heart and give us a heart of flesh. This new Spirit, the Holy Ghost, would give us the power we would need to walk in the statutes and keep the judgments of God through the born again experience.

When did this happen? God gave us instructions on how to be born again in the book of Acts on the Day of Pentecost (instructions–Acts 2:38).

In Hebrews 8:8-13, Paul tells the Hebrews how God had made a new covenant and how God had put his laws (Torah – God's teaching and instruction) into the mind of man. And God would write his laws (Torah) in our hearts by the reception of the Holy Spirit as recorded in Peter's first sermon, Acts 2:1-42.

Therefore, Paul said, the old covenant would vanish. Why? Because all of the Law (Torah) have been incorporated into the name and body of Jesus Christ who is the Holy Spirit. The Holy Spirit (Jesus-Yeshua) wrote the commandments on our hearts so we wouldn't sin against Him.

Acts 2:38 is the answer to Nicodemus question to Jesus Christ. How can a man be born again? John 3:3-5. Man is born of the water by the baptism in the name of Jesus Christ and he is born of the Spirit by the reception of the Holy Spirit.

The Old Testament point forward to the cross in Acts 2:38 and the New Testament sermon in Acts 2:38 points back to the cross to show the operation of God's Word through the cross. The fulfillment of the Law (Torah – God's teaching and instruction) and the culmination of God's Word were carried out through his apostles. If the Seventh Day Adventist could see how God has incorporated his Sabbath into the body of Jesus Christ, then they will understand how the Sabbath was used in salvation through the use of God's name and the Holy Ghost.

The Sabbath has been applied to the mind, hearts, and souls of men by the reception of God's Holy Spirit who is Jesus Christ in his Spirit form. The only way we can remember the Sabbath and keep it Holy is by the reception of the Holy Spirit which is the power of God (Exodus 20:8). We cannot keep the Sabbath Holy without the Spirit of God. In summary, we are complete in him (Colossians 2:8-12).

Today we have present truth. We can remember the Sabbath and keep it Holy by understanding what transpired in Jerusalem and getting an understanding of Peter's sermon in Acts (Acts 2:1-38). This is the fulfillment of the Sabbath day by God himself. Therefore, one should hold tenaciously to the Sabbath which is now Jesus Christ, the Holy Spirit, the fulfillment of the Law (Torah – God's teaching and instruction).

We must be careful because Jesus Christ and the apostles admonished us not to judge our brothers concerning any holydays or Sabbaths because we will become judges to our own hurt. If one tries to admonish their brothers without understanding God's Word, we might be persecuting saints of God without the knowledge of who God is and the true meaning of the Sabbath (John 5:16, 9:14-16, Acts 18:12-15).

There was a great transformation on the day of Pentecost. The Sabbath, which God put in our hearts, is not limited to just one day of the week any more. The Sabbath has become a part of our everyday lives because God placed the Sabbath in our mind and in our hearts by the reception of the Holy Spirit. Therefore we take the Sabbath with us where ever we go (Hebrews 8:8-13). No one can judge a child of God concerning days or Sabbaths.

Those Christian believers, who have put on Christ through repentance, baptism in the name of Jesus Christ for remission of sins and have received the gift of his Spirit, can choose any day to worship God because we have the law (Torah – God's teaching and instruction) and the Sabbath is in our inward parts. God says, "For where two or three are gathered together in my name, there am I in the midst of them" (Matthew 18:20, James 4:10-12, Colossians 2:8-23, I Corinthians 4:1-6, Romans 14:10-13).

Therefore, if a child of God who has been born again according to Acts 2:38, chooses a day to worship, bid him God's speed because he has the Spirit of God and the Sabbath is with him (Colossians 2:8-12, 16). One should never judge or be critical of another brother because of his days and times of worship. The scriptures tell us we should work out our own soul salvation.

Paul said. in I Corinthians 1:10, "Now I beseech you, brethren, by the name of our Lord Jesus Christ, that ye all speak the same thing and that there be no divisions among you; but that ye be perfectly joined together in the same mind and in the same judgment".

I don't advocate all Christian organizations form a world religion or world church. Christians should understand the oneness of God, the power of his name, the Torah, the Sabbath, salvation, and the mystery of Jesus Christ.

The gospel and the revelation and knowledge of Jesus Christ have its roots in Acts 2:38. Once we understand the full ramifications of this scripture, we will understand the full gospel, and the culmination of the plan of salvation.

In terms of most Christian denominations; I realize there will be many who will not believe the true gospel of Jesus Christ. They won't listen nor search the scriptures for themselves because they are steeped in the traditions of men and they can't see the power of God's name in the scriptures. Jesus Christ (Yeshua) is the fullness of God and the power of his Word (John 1:1, 14, Colossians 2:9-10).

There are some followers of Christ who have eyes that can't see and ears that can't hear what the Spirit is saying to the church. However, I believe, by the power of God, he will bring a people out of a people from every denomination and he will reveal to them the knowledge and mystery of his name and the true gospel message of salvation.

Some will believe and be saved while others will hold on to their philosophies and traditions of men and be lost because they were not able to see the revelation of Jesus Christ. They will be lost because of their unbelief in the Word of God. The thing that's unfortunate is they won't recognize they are lost and they won't realize they don't believe God's Word. They will feel they are ok with their own philosophies and traditions. We can do everything we can to show them the mystery of the gospel message and the keys of the kingdom of heaven but unless the Holy Spirit reveals salvation to them, they will never see how the name of Jesus Christ was used in the plan of salvation.

We must not forget II Timothy 4:3-4. For the time will come when they will not endure sound doctrine; but after their own lusts shall they heap to themselves teachers, having itching ears; And they shall turn away their ears from the truth, and shall be turned unto fables. The Trinity, the three co-equal persons in the Godhead, is a fable and is not true. God is one Lord not three persons

Remember the Pharisees and Sadducees. They also held on to their traditional doctrines concerning the Sabbath, which they didn't understand, therefore, they missed the only God of heaven and earth, The Lord of the Sabbath, Jesus Christ (Matthew 12:8). Jesus Christ was the fulfillment of the Sabbath and God personally put the Sabbath in our mind and wrote it on our hearts by the reception of his Holy Spirit (Jeremiah 31:31-33, Ezekiel 36:26-27).

If we are not careful, we will find it will be easy to fall into another philosophy and tradition of men which speaks of the three persons of God which will cause one to fall into error and reprobation. And we will never understand Jesus Christ was in the Old Testament as the Word, which was and is the Spirit of God. For Jews to understand the three manifestations of God from a Christian's perspective, I have enclosed a letter I wrote to my Jewish Christian friend. This letter explains the oneness of God, the name, and salvation from a Oneness Christians' perspective.

"Jesus is Lord (Yeshua is Yahweh)"
(Gen. 17:1, Deut. 6:4, Isa. 9:6, 43:11, Luke 2:11,
John 1:10, 8:24, 58, Titus 2:13, Rev. 1:7-8)

CHAPTER 27

ONE GOD, THE NAME, AND SALVATION

Letter to my Jewish friend

This statement should accompany this letter. Will Daniels, Author of *"Understanding the Oneness of God And the Conspiracy against Jesus Christ and the Christian Church,"* gives permission to copy this letter only, not the entire book which would violate copyright laws. The letter is self explanatory and needs no other personal or written interpretation by any person or organization. The letter can be used as a witness to family, friends, and acquaintances. You can help us spread the gospel of Jesus Christ around the world by using this letter as a witness.

Today, God is revealing his oneness, the power of his name, and salvation through a oneness of God theology, which brings us back to the original gospel message of one God, the name, and salvation.

The foundation of God's oneness is in this statement. "Hear, O Israel: The Lord our God is one Lord" (Deuteronomy 6:4). Now, how do we relate this statement to God's name and salvation in the New Testament? We relate the name in the New Testament by understanding there are not three persons in one God. God manifested or revealed himself in many forms to communicate with man (Hebrews 1:1-3, 8).

God is one God and One Person, who revealed himself as three manifestations for the salvation of man. Again, the key word is "manifestations" of the Father, the Son and the Holy Spirit (I Timothy 3:16, I John 1:1-2). Many people in the New Testament era thought of Jesus Christ as a teacher, rabbi, and/or prophet, not realizing he was God himself. Jesus Christ is Yahweh. Jesus Christ was Yahweh in his Spirit form before He became flesh. We must understand Jesus Christ is the same God (Yahweh) who spoke to Abraham, Isaac, and Jacob (John 1:1, 10, 14. Exodus 3:14, John 8:58).

In addition, Jesus Christ is the God who spoke to Moses and led the children of Israel out of Egypt. Therefore there are not three persons in one God. There is only One God and Jesus Christ is that One God. There is no other name whereby we must be saved (Acts 4:12, I Corinthians 10:4, Acts 9:5).

The beginning of the understanding of the salvation message came when Nicodemus asked Jesus Christ the question about being born again (John 3:1-8). Let's use this scripture as the foundation. Jesus Christ said, except a man is born of water and of the Spirit, he cannot enter into the Kingdom of God. This born again scripture was carried out by Peter in the book of Acts. Peter and the words he spoke are very important in the plan of salvation.

Jesus wanted Peter to understand who he was by asking Peter in Matthew 16:13-19, who did he think he was? Peter told Jesus he was the Christ, meaning: Jesus Christ is God (Yahweh) himself manifested in the flesh. Jesus explained he was correct and told him he would build his Church upon this rock. (Psalm 18:31, I Corinthians 10:4, Acts 2:38).

What was the rock Jesus was referring to in Matthew 16:18? Jesus Christ was referring to his name and the knowledge and mystery of Jesus Christ; "The Rock". In other words, when Jesus Christ said, "upon this rock I will build my Church, he is saying because you have received the knowledge of who I am from the Spirit of God, I will build my church upon my name by baptism. The rock is the baptism in Jesus name and the gates of hell shall not prevail against it (Matthew 16:18, Acts 2:38).

In other words, the church is built on the mystery of the name of Jesus Christ, which can only be revealed by the Spirit of God and not by flesh and blood (man). Jesus asked Peter who he was because the only way one could proclaim the true message of Jesus Christ is; you must know him.

If you don't know Jesus Christ, you can't effectively preach the gospel. Man, which is flesh and blood, can't explain the mystery of Christ to you. You will only receive the mystery of Christ from the Spirit of God. Therefore, salvation is built on the mystery and knowledge of the name of Jesus Christ. The words of Peter would confirm and establish the name of Jesus Christ and the mystery of baptism, which saves, and is the mystery of the rock of our salvation. These same words would represent and become the keys of the kingdom of heaven which were given to Peter. (I Peter 3:21, Colossians 3:17).

Salvation is based on the keys of the kingdom of heaven and the rock which was included in the words. The words which would be spoken by Peter opened the door to the Church. The rock is the baptism in the name of Jesus Christ; for remission of sins because there is no other name under heaven given among men, whereby we must be saved (Acts 2:38, 4:12).

Therefore, the foundation and rock of our salvation spoken by Peter would be honored by God as the salvation message whether Peter loosed, (released, permitted, said) it in heaven or on earth. To validate what I'm saying, let's go to the book of Acts 2:36-39 to get a better understanding of;

1. The question Nicodemus asked Jesus Christ – answered (John 3:5, Acts 2:38)
2. How to be born again – answered (Matthew 28:19, Acts 2:38)
3. How the name Jesus Christ, the Rock, was used in baptism (Matt. 16:18, Acts 2:38, I Cor. 10:4)
4. How the Keys were used to open the door to the Church – answered (Matthew 16:19, Acts 2:38)
5. The importance of God's name and how it is used in salvation – answered (Matt. 28:19, Acts 2:38)
6. How to get remission of sins by the washing of the blood (water) – answered (John 3:5, Acts 2:38)
7. How to understand the reception of the Holy Ghost (Spirit) – answered (John 3:5, Acts 2:38, 19:1-5)

To understand what Jesus Christ told Nicodemus, one must understand how to be born of the water and Spirit. One should be baptized in water in the name of Jesus Christ, the rock upon which the church is built, for remission of sins, and receive the gift of the Holy Spirit. The born again scripture is satisfied in the words of Peter (John 3:5, Acts 2:38). In this scripture, Acts 2:38, we see how Peter used the keys of the kingdom of heaven to open the door to the Church of Jesus Christ. The keys of the kingdom of heaven that were given to Peter in Matthew 16:19 are;

1st **Key** Repentance (613 Principles) Luke 24:47
2nd **Key** Baptism in the name of Jesus Christ for remission of sins (water - John 3:5)
3rd **Key** Receive the gift of the Holy Ghost (Spirit - John 3:5)

These words spoken by Peter became the rock of our salvation which is based on the name, the water, and the Spirit of Christ. The name spoken by Peter is the rock Jesus Christ was talking about in Matthew 16:18. Jesus Christ built the Church upon the rock which is his name in baptism. That name, rock, was spoken by Peter and God assures us the gates of hell would not prevail against it; for there is none other name under heaven given among men, whereby we must be saved (Psalm 18:31, I Corinthians 10:4, Acts 4:12).

One must be baptized in the name of Jesus Christ, the rock to receive the washing of the blood and remission of sins by the water and the Spirit of Jesus Christ. This is what Jesus had promised Nicodemus when he referred to the water and Spirit in John 3:5.

Now, let's go to baptism and why we should baptize in the name of Jesus Christ. In Matthew 28:18-19, Jesus Christ told the apostles before his ascension that all power was given to him in heaven and in earth. In other words, I'm God, all power is in my hand and you should go and teach all nations, baptizing them in the name of the Father, and of the Son, and of the Holy Ghost. This scripture was satisfied by the words of Peter in Acts 2:38. Peter didn't baptize in God's titles, Father, Son and Holy Ghost as one would suppose. Peter did exactly what Jesus Christ told him to do. He baptized new converts in "the name," of Jesus Christ, God's name (Colossians 2:8-12, Revelation 1:7-8)

In order to be "born again" of the water and of the Spirit, one must repent, be baptized in Jesus' name for remission of sins and receive the Holy Ghost, which is a gift from God. To understand salvation, the name, and the born again experience, we will have to understand how to be born again by using God's name mentioned in Matthew 28:19, Acts 2:38, and Acts 4:12. We can see the power is in the name of Jesus Christ (The Torah, The Shema, and The rock). Let's review;

1. The name of the **Father** is Jesus Christ (Isaiah 9:6, 14:9)
2. The name of the **Son** is Jesus Christ (Matthew 1:21-23, Mark 1:1, Galatians 4:4)
3. The name of the **Holy Spirit** is Jesus Christ (John 14:26, Romans 8:9-11)

Therefore, the rock of our salvation spoken by Peter is the baptism in the name of Jesus Christ and Nicodemus' question about how to be born again was fulfilled at the same time (John 3:5 and Acts 2:38).

The born again scripture was satisfied in Acts 2:38. The only way one will understand the baptism in the name of Jesus Christ, is by understanding the Shema, Hear O Israel: The Lord our God is One Lord. And that one Lord is revealed as Jesus Christ who is the rock of our salvation and we are saved through his name by baptism, for there is no other name given among men whereby we must be saved (Acts 4:12).

Study the book of Acts and you will see Paul and the apostles always baptized in the name of the Lord Jesus Christ for salvation and the remission of sins. The remission of sins was after baptism because sins are washed away by the blood. The baptism in the name of Jesus Christ came before and sometimes after the reception of the Holy Spirit. Baptism in Jesus name is absolutely necessary for salvation for there is no other name given among men whereby we must be saved. (Acts 4:12, Colossians 3:17, I Peter 3:21).

This is the baptismal formula I have used in the past after "a new convert" had repented. Just before I baptize the person, I would say;

My dearly beloved brother/sister. Upon the confession of your faith in the death, burial and resurrection of our Lord and Saviour Jesus Christ and the confidence we have in the blessed Word of God. I now baptize you in the name of Our Lord and Saviour Jesus Christ, for the remission of sins, and you shall receive the gift of the Holy Ghost.

After the baptism, I would tell the convert all of your sins have been washed away and everything you have done in your past life has been forgiven and you can start your life over just as if you were a brand new baby. God bless you, stay in church and live a Holy and sanctified life. (a true witness of Jesus Christ)

This is the end of the Letter.

"Jesus is Lord (Yeshua is Yahweh)"
(Gen. 17:1, Deut. 6:4, Isa. 9:6, 43:11, Luke 2:11,
John 1:10, 8:24, 58, Titus 2:13, Rev. 1:7-8)

CHAPTER 28

A TRUE WITNESS OF JESUS CHRIST

There is a conspiracy against true witnesses of Jesus Christ. Who are the true witnesses of our Lord and Saviour Jesus Christ? The true witnesses of God believe in the monotheism/oneness of God; one Supreme Being, and the understanding there is only one Person in the Godhead.

True witnesses believe God was manifested in the flesh and he is the one and only true God. True witnesses believe Jesus Christ is the "I am he," they believe Jesus Christ is "I am," and they believe Jesus Christ is the only Saviour (Exodus 3:14, Isaiah 43:10-11, John 8:24-28, 58, 1 John 5:20).

Let's look at Isaiah 43:10-11. ye are my witnesses, saith the Lord, and my servant whom I have chosen; that ye may know and believe me, and understand that "I am he" before me there was no God formed, neither shall there be after me. I, even I, am the Lord; and beside me there is no saviour.

If we have knowledge of the New Testament, Isaiah 40:3 and Matthew 3:3 tell us Jesus Christ is the Lord and God who will come to the earth. The voice of him that crieth in the wilderness, prepare ye the way of the Lord, make straight in the desert a highway for our God. These scriptures are extremely clear. Isaiah, being a Jew, who believes in one God, calls Jesus Christ our God, even though he didn't know God's highest name at the time of his prophecy.

Jesus Christ fits all the aforementioned scriptures as the one true God. Again, you are going to find in this book a number of things which seem to be redundant, but they are redundant with a purpose in mind. The purpose is to continuously wash your mind with God's Word so you might get a clearer understanding of God's manifestations and to help you learn and remember these scriptures when you finish reading the book. These scriptures will help you in your prayer and meditation. God will make his Word clearer to you if you would diligently seek him. You must leave your traditions behind and be open to truth.

All scriptures will lead back to the validation of Jesus Christ as God, how his identity relates to his human form, the method of salvation, and how to be born again. If you will notice, you will find in all of the referenced scriptures there is a conscious effort to show who Jesus Christ is; the oneness of God, his manifestations, and the scriptural meanings in relation to salvation. In other words, the whole foundation of salvation is based on the oneness of God, the mystery of Jesus Christ and the application of the gospel.

The following conversation with Nicodemus helps us focus on the gospel message as it relates to the New Testament. Nicodemus asked Jesus Christ how he could enter into the kingdom of heaven. Jesus told Nicodemus except a man be born of the water and of the Spirit, he cannot enter into the kingdom of God. As we know, Nicodemus was perplexed and he really didn't understand what Jesus was saying. Nicodemus didn't know Jesus was speaking of a prophetic event. The actual method of being born again with the water and the Spirit was carried out by Peter who had the keys of the kingdom of heaven (John 3:5, Matthew 16:19, Acts 2:38).

In order to understand how to be born again, one would have to know the identity of Jesus Christ. You will have to understand what Jesus Christ said in Matthew 28:19 and what Peter said in Acts 2:38. The only way you will understand the baptism in the name of Jesus Christ will be by study and revelation through the Spirit of Christ. The name of the Father, Son, and Holy Ghost is Jesus Christ (Colossians 2:9).

In Acts 2:38, the keys in Matthew 16:19 were used to open the door to the kingdom of God. If you can't find Jesus Christ, then you can't open the door with the keys. I've come to realize unless you know Jesus Christ, you will be just as perplexed as Nicodemus concerning the name, water and Spirit.

One must know Jesus Christ in order to understand the logic of being "born again" as spoken by Peter. Unbelievers don't know they don't know how to be "born again". They don't know Jesus Christ is the everlasting Father and the Almighty God. Therefore they get lost in philosophies and fables because they won't believe the baptism in the name of Jesus Christ is the door and rock upon which our salvation is built (I Corinthians 10:4, Matthew 16:18).

Most Christians don't realize they don't believe in God's Word. Unbelievers try to prove the Bible wrong according to their own understanding. They have the spirit of the antichrist. They are against Christ. They don't know the mystery of God, therefore, if the gospel is hid, it is hid from those that are lost.

Most unbelievers don't believe in the monotheism of God (Complete oneness of God-Single Person-with no other persons involved). They don't believe in the Bible without some personal or traditional interpretations.

For example;

- Isaiah 9:6 —They don't believe Jesus Christ is the Mighty God and the Everlasting Father.

- John 1:1, 10—They don't believe Jesus Christ is the God who created heaven and earth

- Isaiah 43:10—They don't believe God is our Saviour Jesus Christ

- Revelation 1:7-8—They don't believe Jesus Christ when he said, he's the Almighty.

- I Timothy 3:16, John 1:1, 14—They don't believe Jesus Christ is God in the flesh.

- Acts 2:38, 10:48, 22:16, 19:1-5—They don't believe baptism in the name of Jesus Christ.

- Exodus 3:14—They don't believe Jesus Christ is "I am" John 8:58.

- John 14:7-10—They don't believe Jesus Christ when he said he is the everlasting Father.

- I John 5:43—They don't believe Jesus Christ came in his Father's name.

- I Corinthians 10:4—They don't believe God's name is Jesus Christ (Acts 9:5).

- I John 5:20—They don't believe Jesus Christ is the only true God.

- II Corinthians 5:19—They don't believe God was in Jesus Christ

- Colossians 1:19, 2:8-12—They don't believe Jesus is the Father, Son, and Holy Ghost.

Some believe another Saviour was formed in the person of Jesus Christ (the Son), whom they don't recognize as God the Father - Jesus Christ (Isaiah 9:6, John 14:6-9, Colossians 2:8-9, II Corinthians 5:19).

God himself spoke to Saul while Saul was on the road to Damascus When God identified himself as Jesus Christ, Saul became one of God greatest evangelist because there was no doubt in his heart and mind Jesus Christ was the one Lord God Almighty, the God of Abraham, Isaac and Jacob. Once you have a clear understanding of who Jesus really is; you will have a burning desire to spread your renewed understanding of the gospel to the world. (Acts 9:4-5, I Corinthians 10:4).

A key point to remember is all unbelief is centered on either the belief or unbelief in Jesus name and the understanding that Jesus Christ is God himself (I Corinthians 10:4, Acts 9:5).

What's important is every unbeliever must question his own logic; if he/she starts to believe in more than one person in God, or start to believe Jesus Christ is not the one God; then their thinking is in error. If there is any one scripture he/she does not believe without some secret or traditional interpretation, then he/she is an unbeliever. Our logic and understanding is in error if we don't agree with the scriptures the way they are written.

If a person is sincere and really wants to acquire the knowledge of Jesus Christ, he/she should do more research and they will come to the same conclusion. Jesus Christ is the one and only true God of heaven and earth (1 John 5:20).

The preceding scriptures are true and they can be understood plainly and without interpretation. They will affirm the monotheism of God is true and the doctrine of the Trinity is suspect. The Trinity is a doctrine that's difficult to understand and the scriptures can't prove it. And since this doctrine is so difficult to understand, we need to know where the Trinity came from? Research the origin of the Trinity in your local Public Library.

Now, it's your time to do some research on your own. Make no mistake about it; I want you to see God is one God, and he has always been one and still is one. God himself came down as a manifestation of His Spirit. Remember "Jesus is Lord" and there is only one Lord. Jesus Christ is the same God, in his Spirit form, as the Word, who talked to Abraham, Isaac and Jacob, and the prophets in the Old Testament (I Corinthians 10:4, Acts 9:5).

Jesus Christ is the Messiah, a manifestation of the one God (Spirit), who created the world. God walked among us and we didn't know him. Jesus Christ is the Father, the Son, and the Holy Spirit. There are three manifestations of one God, not three persons. Study and you will get the same understanding of the mystery of Jesus Christ. Don't lean on your own traditional understanding and interpretations. (John 1:1-15, Colossians 2:8-12, I John 1:1-2).

There is only one "God the Father" whose name is Jesus Christ according to all the scriptures in both the Old and New Testaments. Jesus Christ is the one and only True and Living God. We can prove Jesus Christ is God and we can prove there is a conspiracy by well meaning Christians who unknowingly make antichrist statements.

"Jesus is Lord (Yeshua is Yahweh)"
(Gen. 17:1, Deut. 6:4, Isa. 9:6, 43:11, Luke 2:11,
John 1:10, 8:24, 58, Titus 2:13, Rev. 1:7-8)

CHAPTER 29

ANTICHRIST STATEMENTS AGAINST JESUS CHRIST

There is a conspiracy against Jesus Christ by Christians who are unaware they are participating in a satanic conspiracy to destroy the Word of God by making antichrist statements.

When Jesus made a statement which would ensure salvation; the spirit of the antichrist would say something to this effect," that's not necessary to be saved". Let's take a look at some of the antichrist statements some Christians unknowingly proclaim to the world as truth.

1. Antichrist statement: Jesus Christ is not God the Father.

Not True: Jesus Christ is God the Father (Isaiah 9:6, John 14:6-9)

2. Antichrist statement: Jesus Christ is not the one Lord God Almighty.

Not True: Jesus Christ is the one Lord God Almighty. (Genesis 17:1, Revelation 1:7-8)

3. Antichrist statement: There are three persons in One God

Not True: There are three manifestations of one God (I Tim. 3:16, 1 John 1:1-2)

4. Antichrist statement: God is a triune being.

Not true*:* God is one Person with many attributes not two other persons with him (Deut. 6:4)

5. Antichrist statement: Jesus Christ is not Jehovah the Almighty

Not True: Jesus Christ is Jehovah the Almighty (Genesis 17:1, Rev.1:8)

6. Antichrist statement: Jesus Christ is not the Holy Ghost

Not True: Jesus Christ is the Holy Ghost (John 14:6, 17, 18)

7. Antichrist statement: Jesus Christ and God are not the same Person.

Not True: Jesus and God is the same Person (I Corinthians 10:4, John 10:30, Hebrews 1:3)

8. Antichrist statement: God is not one Person.

Not True: God is one Person-Jesus Christ (John 1:10, II Cor. 5:19, Col. 1:19, 2:9, Heb. 1:3)

9. Antichrist statement: God is a Trinity of three persons

Not True: The Trinity is an assumption; God is one Person (Job 13:6-11, Heb. 1:3)

10. Antichrist statement: Jesus Christ is the second person in the Godhead.

Not True: Jesus Christ is the only Person in the Godhead (Matt. 1:23, Col. 2:8-9, Rev. 1:7-8)

11. Antichrist statement: Jesus Christ is not the God of heaven and earth.

Not True: Jesus Christ is the God of heaven and earth (Matthew 28:18, Rev. 1:7-8)

12. Antichrist statement: Jesus Christ is not the Father; he is only the Son

Not True: Jesus is the Father and Son of God (Isaiah 9:6, John 14:6-9, Matthew 16:16)

13. Antichrist statement: The Holy Ghost is the third person in the Trinity.

Not true: God never said He is a third person—God is one Person (Job 13:1-11, Heb. 1:3)

14. Antichrist statement: You don't need to be baptized to be saved.

Not True: Jesus Christ said; you must be baptized to be saved (Mark 16:16)

15. Antichrist statement: Confess with your mouth; you are saved (no water, no Spirit)

Not True: The true salvation scripture is Acts 2:38. Water and Spirit (John 3:5)

16. Antichrist statement: There are two baptisms, Matt. 28:19, Acts 2:38, either one is ok.

Not True: There is only one baptism (Ephesians 4:5, Acts 2:38, 10:48, 19:1-5)

17. Antichrist statement: The prophets in the Old Testament didn't speak to Christ.

Not True: Jesus "the Christ," is the Rock that spoke to the prophets (I Cor. 10:4)

    18. Antichrist statement: Jesus Christ is not as powerful as God the Father.

Not True: Jesus is God the Father with all power in heaven and earth (Matt 28:18, Rev. 1:7-8)

    19. Antichrist statement: Jesus "the Christ" never spoke out of heaven as God.

Not True: Jesus Christ spoke out of heaven as God "the Christ" (I Cor. 10:4, Acts 9:5)

    20. Antichrist statement: The Trinity is a monotheistic religion.

Not True: The Trinity believes in three persons in God which is paganism, not monotheism.

    21. Antichrist statement: The three manifestations of God is heresy (Church history)

Not True: Three manifestations of God are proven and not heresy (I Tim. 3:16, I John 1:1-2)

    22. Antichrist statement: Jesus is another Person other than God the Father.

Not True: Jesus Christ is the only Person in heaven (Deut. 6:4, Luke 2:11)

    23. Antichrist statement: You don't have to do everything in Jesus Christ name

Not True: Christians must do everything in the name of the Lord Jesus (Colossians 3:17)

24. Antichrist statement: Jesus Christ is a lessor or subordinate god.

Not True: Jesus Christ is the only God (Gen 17:1, John 1:10, I Cor. 10:4, Rev.1:8)

25. Antichrist statement: Nobody said Jesus Christ is the everlasting Father.

Not True: The prophet Isaiah said Jesus is the everlasting Father (Isaiah 9:6)

26. Antichrist statement: Jesus Christ never said He is the Father.

Not True: Jesus said, if you have seen me you have seen the Father (John 14:6-9)

27. Antichrist statement: Jesus Christ never said He is the Almighty.

Not True: Jesus Christ tells us He is the Almighty (Acts 9:1-5, Revelation 1:7-8)

28. Antichrist statement: Jesus Christ is not the one Lord and God.

Not True: Jesus is the one Lord and God (Deut. 6:4, Luke 2:11, John 20:28, Eph. 4:5-6)

29. Antichrist statement: You can be saved without water baptism.

Not True: Baptism saves (Mark 16:16, I Peter 3:21)

30. Antichrist statement: Baptism in the name of Jesus Christ is not necessary.

Not True: Baptism in the name of Jesus Christ is the Rock upon which the church is built and the gates of hell shall not prevail against the baptism in the name of Jesus Christ – the Rock (Psalm 18:31, Matthew 16:18, 28:19, Acts 2:38, 19:5, Romans. 6:3-4, I Corinthians 10:4, Colossians 2:12, 3:17).

If any person, theologian, teacher, preacher or any such person challenges the Word of God, he is an antichrist, not understanding nor rightly dividing the Word of God. Remember, you are not fighting against my writings; you are challenging the Word of God and the scriptures presented for your edification.

The confusion of not understanding the scriptures, the operation of God, and his three manifestations can only be understood by those who believe in the absolute oneness of God. If you believe God is three persons, you will never see the operation and mystery of Jesus Christ nor will you understand the gospel of salvation. You will never understand how to be born again, you won't understand how the keys of the kingdom were used, you will never understand how salvation is built upon the rock through baptism in the name of Jesus Christ, and you will never understand what Jesus Christ said about the commission and how it was to be carried out by the apostles in Acts. Salvation and the great commission are based on doctrinal truth. But what is doctrinal truth?

"Jesus is Lord (Yeshua is Yahweh)"
(Gen. 17:1, Deut. 6:4, Isa. 9:6, 43:11, Luke 2:11,
John 1:10, 8:24, 58, Titus 2:13, Rev. 1:7-8)

CHAPTER 30

DOCTRINAL TRUTH

What is the conspiracy against doctrinal truth? We can answer this question by asking a question. What do Vick's vapor rub and this book about the oneness of God have in common? The doctrinal truths presented here, like Vick's vapor rub, will open up your mind and understanding to the mystery of Jesus Christ, the oneness of God, and how this one God was manifested as a man – Jesus Christ (I Timothy 3:16).

In order to understand doctrinal truth, we have to destroy some of the myths that have slowly crept into the Christian church. Some myths have been with the church so long they have been accepted and adopted by most Christian organizations as truth, even though, those concepts are not in the Bible and cannot be proven by scripture.

In my last book, "*Understanding the Trinity, Three Persons vs Three Manifestations*," I talk about going through "a paradigm shift".

In 1962, Thomas Kuhn, a graduate of Harvard University wrote a book called, "The Structure of Scientific Revolution" and coined the term "paradigm shift". In order to find truth we must be willing to go through a "paradigm shift" as Mr. Kuhn suggests.

> *According to www.taketheleap.com, "think of a paradigm shift as a change from one way of thinking to another. It's a revolution, a*

> *transformation, a sort of metamorphosis. It just does not happen,*
> *but rather it is driven by agents of change".*

My understanding of *a paradigm shift is the realization that a thing, event,*
theory, or concept is true after the facts have presented themselves".

I'm going to present some Biblical facts so you will go through your own
personal paradigm shift to find the truth of Jesus Christ and the Christian
Church. To prove a point, let me give you a scenario passed down over the
years. I don't know where it came from.

This is the question. What would you say if I asked you; would you jump
out of an airplane without a parachute for one million dollars? Would you
do it? You probably would say, "no way". Well, suppose I asked you again
but this time I would say, would you jump out of an airplane without a
parachute for $10 million dollars, would you do it? The answer would
probably still be an emphatic, "no way".

Now, I'm going to ask you again, and give your more information. Would
you jump out of an airplane for $1 million dollars, without a parachute, if
the plane was on the ground? Would you do it? Now, your answer would
be yes, yes, yes, of course I would. Now, why would you do it? You would
do it because I would have given you more information.

In summary, your new answer of "yes" would have taken the additional
facts into consideration. Now, we have changed an emphatic "no" into
our new answer-an emphatic "yes". That change in answers is called a
"paradigm shift". When you have more facts, your understanding and your
answer will change. In other words, you are forced to change your answer
based on the facts.

Paradigm shifts are not unusual. These type shifts are experienced on a
regular basis by doctors, lawyers, judges, scientists, teachers, theologians,
etc. Once the facts have presented themselves, no matter what you once
believed as truth in the past, you must go with the facts which created a
new understanding of what truth is - a paradigm shift.

I want you to remember this paradigm shift scenario when I present Christian facts about the gospel and the saving grace of our Lord and Saviour Jesus Christ. Your early Christian training and traditions will be challenged after the facts have presented themselves. Go with the paradigm shift which will lead you into the truth of Jesus Christ. (Isaiah 43:10-11, Luke 2:11, Titus 2:13).

There have been a number of Christian truths missed and/or misinterpreted because we have not gathered all of the facts. We have taken someone's word for Christian truths and we have not challenged the concepts which changed Christianity to the doctrine of the Trinity over the centuries. Why haven't we challenged the Trinity? We didn't challenge the Trinity because we didn't understand it. We should ignore these errant Christian concepts and conspiracies against Jesus Christ and start over with the original doctrine of the apostles (Acts 2:42).

The Lord has given us the facts through his Word. Once the facts of the gospel message have presented themselves, you too will have a paradigm shift about the knowledge, mystery, and true nature of Jesus Christ. Truth is always a little scary when our traditional understandings have been challenged. For some, change is extremely difficult.

However, I would like to suggest you go with the flow and the paradigm shift in God's Word and you can't go wrong. Jesus Christ is light and there is no darkness in Him at all. Don't trust the things I say or what anyone else says. Trust God's Word and see how the knowledge and mystery of Jesus Christ will unfold before your own eyes.

Think of a blind man you have taken by the hand to lead him in a direction of your choice. That blind man would have to put his full trust in you. He must believe you would not take him in an area where he is not safe. You must do the same with the gospel of Jesus Christ. You must go through a paradigm shift of doctrinal truths using the Word of God as your guide. Jesus Christ will not leave nor forsake you. God's Word is light and truth and you will feel this solid truth of Jesus Christ come into your own life through the revealed Word of God.

Will Daniels

In order to properly spread the gospel of Jesus Christ to the world, we must, as Christians, have an understanding of the mystery of Jesus Christ and we must be of one mind and be on one accord (I Corinthians 1:9).

We must understand the mystery of Jesus Christ and doctrinal truth concerning his death, burial, and resurrection and how the power of God's name was used in salvation. In order to find truth doctrinal truth, we must eliminate the belief in the Trinitarian Doctrine.

"Jesus is Lord (Yeshua is Yahweh)"
(Gen. 17:1, Deut. 6:4, Isa. 9:6, 43:11, Luke 2:11,
John 1:10, 8:24, 58, Titus 2:13, Rev. 1:7-8)

CHAPTER 31

THE TRINITARIAN DOCTRINE

The Trinitarian doctrine is not in the Bible. The only doctrine mentioned in the Bible which relates to salvation are the apostles' doctrine (Acts 2:42), the doctrine of Christ (II John 1:9), the doctrine of baptisms (Hebrews 6:2), and the doctrine of God (Titus 2:10). All of these doctrinal terms can be used when discussing the doctrine of Jesus Christ. The Trinitarian Doctrine is a doctrine of men created by the Catholic Church (Nicene Council AD 325, 381).

Over the years we have been taught by our parents and elders either you believe in the Bible or you don't believe it, there is no in between. Suppose I told you Jesus Christ is the only true God, the Father of all creation. Would you believe it or would you not believe it? Would that be shocking to you? Guess what; we have proven the Deity of Jesus Christ using the scriptures. The Deity of Jesus Christ (Yeshua HaMashiach) means-Jesus is the one Lord God of Israel (Yahweh) (Deuteronomy 6:4, John 1:1-10, Colossians 1:14-19).

Based on our traditional Trinitarian doctrine, we don't believe Jesus Christ is the everlasting Father according to Isaiah 9:6 John 14:6-9, Acts 9:1-5, and I Corinthians 10:4. Some Christians won't necessarily agree with these scriptures nor will they understand. They want to come up with some type philosophy to try to explain away the Deity and Fatherhood of Jesus Christ. Why? The average Christian doesn't believe the prophet Isaiah when he tells us Jesus Christ is the everlasting Father, nor do we believe Jesus Christ himself when he tells us he is the Father (John 14:6-9).

Now let me show you, as a believer, a paradigm shift in your understanding of the Word of God. Do you believe what Isaiah 9:6 said? You can be a believer in Jesus Christ but not understand the scriptures based on our traditional Trinitarian doctrine. The Trinitarian doctrine tells us Jesus Christ is only the Son of God and not God the Father. You either believe Jesus Christ is the everlasting Father or you don't believe it. There is no in between.

The real truth is; Jesus Christ was the Father in his Spirit form as the Word in the Old Testament and in the New Testament God is the Son in his fleshly or incarnate form. The Word that made heaven and earth was the same Word made flesh in the New Testament. (I Corinthians 10:4, John 1:1, 14).

There is only one Father in the Spirit and one Lord Jesus Christ in the flesh. God is one God who manifested himself in three forms (Father, Son, and Holy Spirit) to work out the salvation of men. (I Corinthians 8:6).

The scriptures are very simple to a believer and can be understood by babes in Christ. However, to an unbeliever or one who thinks that he has all of the wisdom and knowledge of God through his/her own education and doctorial degrees, it's a mystery that they can't see, hear, nor understand.

The first step in believing the true gospel of Jesus Christ is to believe what God has already said. You must believe that Jesus Christ is the Father in order to come to the Father. Jesus Christ said in John 14:6 that no man comes to the Father, but by me. And in verse 7, he says if ye had known me, you should have known my Father also: and from hence forth ye know him, and have seen him.

You can believe Jesus Christ is the everlasting Father because he said he is or you will not believe it because of your traditional Trinitarian doctrinal training. God leaves that up to the individual. But I must warn you; unbelief will cause you to stumble at the entire Word of God. You will never find a solid foundation. And unbelief will eventually lead to disobedience and reprobation (Isaiah 43:10-11, John 8:24).

The Bewilderment of the Trinity: Three Persons vs One Person of God

The Trinitarian Doctrine makes a futile attempt to separate God into 3 distinct persons which is not according to the Word of God. God is one God and he doesn't know of any other gods or persons. God is in one Person according to Job 13:1-11, Colossians 1:19, 2:9, and Hebrews 1:3. Just these scriptures alone prove the Trinitarian Doctrine is a serious violation of scripture. God never told us he is three persons. Three persons in one God is an assumption and a figment of man's imagination. The Trinitarian Doctrine is not mentioned in the Old or the New Testament. The Trinity has nothing to do with a Holy God. (Isaiah 44:6-8).

Most of our major denominations have turned away from the God of Moses, Abraham, Isaac, and Jacob primarily because of the introduction of the Trinitarian Doctrine which was formulated and developed by the Catholic Council of Bishops. The Trinitarian Doctrine which can't be logically understood has caused Christians to fall into a state of apostasy – denying the absolute oneness of God and the Deity of Jesus Christ. Thus, most Christians can't understand the oneness of God and they can't understand the Trinity or the Trinitarian doctrine which is not a sound doctrine. (1Timothy 1:10, 2 Timothy 4:3, Titus 1:9, Titus 2:1). Now, let's take a look at some of the many books written about the Trinity which can't be explained.

Authors who wrote books about the Trinity

J. P. Arendzen, wrote a book called, *"Understanding the Trinity"* which proves the confusion of the Trinity. He writes on page 27

> *"The Blessed Trinity is a mystery in the strictest sense of the word, absolutely beyond the power of unaided human reason".*

Most Christian writers and scholars must admit they don't understand the Trinity as it relates to the oneness of God and the Deity of Jesus Christ. I would venture to say Trinitarian authors can agree there will never be a full understanding of the Trinity because it can't be proven by the Word of God.

Let's take a look at another writer who tries to explain the theological confusions caused by the Trinity.

Millard J. Erickson, wrote a book called, *"Making Sense of the Trinity, Three Crucial Questions,"* In the Introduction, page 13, Mr. Erickson writes,

> *"To those outside the Christian faith, the doctrine of the Trinity seems a very strange teaching indeed. It seems to violate logic, for it claims that God is three and yet that he is one.*

One cannot make any sense of the Trinity. The Trinity violates all logic and understanding of God being three persons. And if we examine the Trinity carefully, we will find the Trinity hinders new converts' understanding of scripture.

Alister E. McGrath wrote in his book, "Understanding the Trinity," pg. 110,

> *"To many people, the doctrine of the Trinity is a piece of celestial mathematics and bad mathematics at that! Why, complained the great rationalist thinkers, should we think of God in so clumsy and complicated a way?*

Jesus Christ is not so complicated He can't be simply understood by his own teachings to the apostles (Acts 2:42). Based on the scriptures, we should just believe God. Jesus Christ is one God without the nonsense of three in one (Genesis 17:1, Revelation 1:7-8).

In my opinion, most Christian writers are just as confused about the Trinity as the average lay person reading their books. Christian writers try to be true to the historical doctrine of the Trinity but the Trinitarian doctrine doesn't fit with true Christian theology. Reason? The Trinity is a manmade doctrine. (Colossians 2:8-9). (Reference the Nicene Council 325AD).

The Trinitarian doctrine can't be Biblically proven. God speaks of himself as absolutely one God in one Person who doesn't council with any other gods or persons (Deuteronomy 32:9, Isaiah 44:6, 8, 45:21, Hebrews 1:3).

No one should tell another Christian to just believe God is three persons when there are no facts to support this type doctrine in the Bible. God never said He is three persons

Paul and the apostles never taught a doctrine of the Trinity, they were dead long before the development of the Trinity in the 4th-5th centuries. (Galatians 1.6-9). To get a better understanding of the historical discussions of the Trinitarian doctrine and the oneness of God, one should read my book, *"Understanding the Trinity, three persons vs Three Manifestations"*. Or go to the Public Library and study the origin of the Trinity. We find in our study of the Trinity there is a conspiracy against the apostles' doctrine..

"Jesus is Lord (Yeshua is Yahweh)"
(Gen. 17:1, Deut. 6:4, Isa. 9:6, 43:11, Luke 2:11,
John 1:10, 8:24, 58, Titus 2:13, Rev. 1:7-8)

CHAPTER 32

THE APOSTLES' DOCTRINE

There is a conspiracy against the Apostles' Doctrine. In order to fully understand the Apostles' doctrine, one must first understand and believe what the scriptures teach about the oneness of God in the Old Testament, "The Shema" (Deuteronomy 6:4). "Hear O Israel: The Lord our God is one Lord:"

The apostles' doctrine (Acts 2:42), the doctrine of Christ (II John 1:9), the doctrine of baptisms (Hebrews 6:2), and the doctrine of God (Titus 2:10) is the same doctrine and are used interchangeably. Most Christian churches like to use the term, doctrine of Christ which is fine.

However, for clarification, let's use the apostles' doctrine in these illustrations. The apostles received their doctrine directly from Christ himself; therefore, the apostles' doctrine is the doctrine of Christ, who is God, thus the doctrine of God which teaches the doctrine of baptism in Jesus name-water and Spirit (John 3:5, Acts 2:38).

John H. Fish III edited a book called, "Understanding the Trinity". He explains in his forward, the essays in his book were a result of oral presentations held on the campus of Emmaus Bible College in Dubuque, Iowa on October 10-12, 2002. The following is a direct statement from Mr. Fish's observation.

"The 2002 symposium on the Trinity arose from our commitment to the belief that the church is to be devoted to the Apostle's teaching (Acts 2:42).

The Christian Church must have a clear and precise understanding of the apostles' doctrine, which comes by seriously studying the scriptures in both the Old and New Testaments concerning the oneness of God.

The doctrine of the Trinity is not in the Bible. The Trinity is a doctrine of men. God never speaks of himself as three persons. The Trinity of one God is a figment of man's imagination. God only spoke of himself as one God and one Spirit in one Person and one body - Jesus Christ. (Colossians 1:19, 2:8-9, Hebrews 1:3, 8). Therefore, we should understand the Trinitarian doctrine vs the apostles' doctrine.

The apostles' doctrine is;

1. The belief in the absolute monotheism of God with no other persons involved. (Deuteronomy 6:4, Isaiah 43:10, 45:21-23, Colossians 2:8-12, Hebrews 1:3).
2. The belief that the grace of God leads to salvation and grace has allowed them to see the light, the understanding, the mystery, and the knowledge of Christ Jesus. (Ephesians 3:1-11, 1 Tim 3:16).
3. The belief that they have faith in the operation of God, his name, and the power of the Holy Ghost (Acts 2:38).
4. The belief that repentance and remission of sins were preached in Jesus name, beginning at Jerusalem. (Luke 24:47, Acts 2:1-42).
5. The belief that Christians will receive power after the Holy Ghost has come upon them to preach the gospel. (Acts 1:8).
6. The belief that if we, or an angel from heaven, preach any other gospel unto you than that which we have preached unto you, let him be accursed. (Galatians 1:6-9).
7. The belief that there is no other name under heaven given among men, whereby we must be saved (Acts 2:38, 4:12).
8. The belief that the "commission" was carried out by Peter on the day of Pentecost. (Matthew 28:19, Acts 2:38).
9. The belief that Jesus Christ is the name mentioned as the Father, Son and Holy Ghost in Matthew 28:19 and that name, Jesus Christ,

is the rock upon which the church is built by baptism in the name of Jesus Christ - God's name (II Samuel 22:32, Matthew 16:18, Acts 2:38, 4:12).

10. The belief that the keys of the kingdom of heaven were spoken by Peter in Acts 2:38. Acts 2:38 is the born again scripture and the method of salvation which is based on repentance, baptism in the name of Jesus Christ for the remission of sins, and the baptism of the Holy Ghost with the evidence of speaking in other tongues as the Spirit gives utterance (John 3:5).

11. The belief that the blood, the death, the burial, and resurrection of our Lord Jesus Christ is applied by baptism in the name of Jesus Christ (Acts 2:38, 8:16, 10:48, 19:5, 22:16, Colossians 2:12, Romans 6:3-4, Mark 16:16). The application of the death, burial and resurrection, and the keys of the kingdom of heaven was carried out by Peter in Acts 2:38 as follows;

    a. **Repentance** - is a death to sin in Jesus name (Yeshua) (Luke 24:47)

    b. **Burial** - is the baptism in Jesus name for remission of sins **(water)** is the rock upon which the church is built – the foundation (Psalm 18:31, Matthew 16:18, Romans 6:3-4, Colossians 2:9-12)

    c. **Resurrection** – the reception of the Holy Ghost in Jesus name **(Spirit)** helps us live a new and resurrected life in the knowledge and mystery of Christ (John 3:5).

12. The belief that Jesus Christ is a manifestation of God (Yahweh) himself (Isaiah 9:6, John 1:1-14, 14:6-9, I Corinthians 10:4, I Timothy 3:16, Titus 2:13, Jude 1:25, Revelation 1:7-8).

The apostles' doctrine is strictly monotheistic in nature. The apostles understood the mystery of the Gospel and the understanding that Jesus Christ was God in Flesh (The promised Messiah–II Corinthians 5:19).

In addition, the apostles understood how to carry out the plan of salvation given by the Lord himself. Peter understood how to use the keys of the kingdom of heaven which were used on the day of Pentecost (Matthew

16:18-19). Peter explained what we needed to do to be saved according to Acts 2:38.

These keys of the kingdom of heaven in Acts 2:38 were used to open the door to the Church of Jesus Christ. The rock of Jesus name baptism is the foundation on which the church is built and has ushered in the doctrine of God, doctrine of baptisms, doctrine of Christ and the apostles' doctrine and the gates of hell (Trinitarian doctrine) shall not prevail against it.

The apostles' doctrine is to be followed by all Christians who want to be saved and who want to understand the mysteries of God. In the book of Acts, we can see how the apostles' doctrine was preached, and how we are to instruct new converts on "how to be born again".

We must say this again, the apostles' doctrine gives us instructions on how to use the great commission, how to be born again, and how to use the keys of the kingdom of heaven which are all culminated in one scripture – Acts 2:38.

Peter's instructions and the keys (613 Torah Principles) of the kingdom of heaven were to; **Key #1.** Repent, confess your sins and turn away from evil. (in my **name** – Luke 24:47)

Key #2. Be baptized in the name of Jesus Christ for remission of sins and the gates of hell shall not prevail against it (rock), which is the name of Jesus Christ, in baptism (the incarnate Torah – Ten Commandments – 613 Principles – Sabbath). Psalm 18:31, Matthew 16:18-19 (the rock), I Corinthians 10:4 (the rock), Matthew 28:19 (Name of the Father and of the Son, and of the Holy Ghost - **water** - John 3:5)

Key #3. You shall receive the gift of the Holy Ghost (Name - Matthew 28:19, - **Spirit**, John 3:5).

As aforementioned, the Oneness of God and how to be born again have been challenged throughout the history of the Christian Church. Doesn't it seem ironic we have to continually prove God is one Lord and one Person in order for one to understand the gospel of salvation? (Deuteronomy 6:4, Job 13:1-11, Hebrews 1:3).

Hopefully, this book God has given us, will give you another way of looking at the oneness of God in the Old Testament and his manifestation as Jesus Christ in the New Testament. Jesus Christ (Yeshua HaMashiach) was in the world, as God. He was in the world, and the world was made by him, and the world knew him not. (John 1:10, I Corinthians 10:4). Most Christians want to know what the true doctrine of Jesus Christ really is.

"Jesus is Lord (Yeshua is Yahweh)"
(Gen. 17:1, Deut. 6:4, Isa. 9:6, 43:11, Luke 2:11,
John 1:10, 8:24, 58, Titus 2:13, Rev. 1:7-8)

Chapter 33

The Doctrine of Jesus Christ

There is a conspiracy against the doctrine of Jesus Christ and the Christian Church. I've always wondered why there are so many factions and doctrine of the Christian faith. I've come to realize there are so many factions of Christianity because of our lack of understanding of the mystery and true doctrine of Jesus Christ concerning salvation. Christians, as a whole, don't understand our own traditions, our own beliefs or unbelief in the Word of God concerning church doctrine, salvation, and the Deity of Jesus Christ.

The Bible is the absolute rock of God's Word, the true doctrinal truth of Jesus Christ, and the foundation of our belief. We have to understand Jesus Christ is our Rock and our God. As Christians we don't see the same things, in the Bible, nor do we have the same understanding that Jesus Christ is the one Lord God Almighty (Psalm 18:31, I Corinthians 10:4, Genesis 17:1, Revelation 1:7-8).

John R.W. Stott wrote in his book, *"Basic Christianity,"* page 21;

> *"There are two principal reasons why our enquiry into Christianity should begin with the person of Christ. The first is that essentially Christianity is Christ. The person and work of Christ are the Rock upon which the Christian religion is built..... Second, if Jesus*

> *Christ can be shown to have been a uniquely divine person, many other problems begin naturally to be solved".*

Jesus Christ is who he said he is. The church is built upon the baptism in the name of Jesus Christ, which is the rock of salvation and the gates of hell shall not prevail against it. (Matthew 16:18-19, Acts 4:12).

When one truly understands who Jesus Christ really is; the mysteries in God's Word will begin to fade away. We are going to give you an insight and an understanding of Jesus Christ as revealed by scripture. Jesus Christ is, as Mr. Stott suggests, the central focus of Christianity and we should strive more diligently to know him.

To get on one accord, let's throw out our own man made traditions and misunderstandings and follow the doctrine of the apostles who had a complete knowledge of the mystery of Jesus Christ (Colossians 2:8-12). The apostles understood what God was saying to the Church and they also understood how to carry out the gospel message of salvation. Let's search the scriptures diligently so we can come to the same conclusion and understanding of the mystery of God and the saving grace of Jesus Christ (Matthew 28:19, Acts 8:16, 10:48, 19:5, 22:16, Romans 6:3-4, Ephesians 4:5, Colossians 2:9-12, I Corinthians 1:10).

Christians have come to believe we have the true doctrine of God because of our belief in the gospel of Jesus Christ and his redemptive work. This is absolutely true according to the New Testament and our understanding of God's Word. However, salvation comes with some caveats. The caveats are the belief or unbelief in the oneness of God, the doctrine of Jesus Christ, the Deity of Jesus Christ, and the belief in the gospel of salvation.

We are caught between following what Jesus said, what the apostles taught or following our own Trinitarian traditions. As Christians, we must be obedient to the Word of God in order to say we are followers of Christ. How can we say we are followers of Christ when we don't understand what God is saying in his Word? Out of all of the different types and beliefs of Christians, which one is right?

One thing we must understand is; all Christians seek truth regardless of their doctrine or religious affiliation. I realize everyone is not going to believe the truths in this book because of the misunderstandings we have with the Word of God. And I also realize people didn't believe the truth as it was taught by Jesus Christ and the apostles when they walked the earth. So why would they believe the truth today?

Some will see the true gospel right away and walk in the light and mystery of Jesus Christ. And there will be others who will have to search the scriptures diligently to find the answers to salvation and be saved. Then there will be others who will feel more comfortable walking in the darkness of their own man made doctrine and traditions.

How did we fall away from the faith as taught by Paul and the apostles? The falling away from the gospel started in Paul's day but the great falling, away, in my opinion, started as a result of a man made document called the Nicene Creed which was first suggested and ratified by the Catholic Church Council of Bishops at the Nicaean Council in 325AD. This Council of Bishops and their agreements were the beginning of the Trinitarian Doctrine and the great falling away from the doctrine of Christ, which has nothing to do with a Trinity.

Constantine put his whole kingdom under this new Trinitarian doctrine of men and declared if anyone challenged this new doctrine they would be ostracized or killed. All churches in his empire were ordered-ordered to adhere to this new Trinitarian doctrine whether they were in agreement with it or not. Any theological thoughts about the absolute oneness of God would have to be discarded and replaced with this new manmade doctrine of the Trinity – three persons in one God.

Constantine, a believer in paganism, called himself a Christian but didn't want to be baptized until just before his death because he wanted to continue sinning. After Constantine said he was a Christian, he had his wife, his son, and his nephew killed. Constantine with his bloody hands agreed with this new Christian doctrine of the Trinity.

This "three person" theory of God had a close relationship with the paganistic and polytheistic practices of that day. Constantine could explain the Trinity to his paganistic/polytheistic believers and get the Roman Catholic Ecumenical Council of Churches to support his proclamations about this new type of Christianity.

Over the centuries, the Nicene Creed which didn't fully support a Trinity, at first, was changed to include an understanding of the Holy Spirit at the Council of Constantinople in 381AD. The Athanasian/Cappadocian formulation which further clarified the Trinitarian doctrine preceded the 381AD Council and gave a better understanding of the theory of three persons in one God.

The Athanasian (Creed) concept of a three person God was adopted at this second ecumenical council at Constantinople. Today, after 6 councils, the Trinitarian Doctrine is taught in most protestant Christian organizations worldwide.

This conspiracy of the Trinitarian Doctrine was developed by men, and agreed to and accepted by Constantine - a pagan. The Trinitarian Doctrine became the doctrine of the Christian church worldwide, even though, the Trinitarian doctrine couldn't be explained nor understood using the Word of God. God never called himself three persons.

The Trinity is a conspiracy and it's not mentioned in the Bible and was never taught by any of the apostles. Paul and the apostles would have been called, in historical terms, Modalists, Sabellianists or Monarchianist (Galatians 1:8-9). Why? Because Paul baptized in the name of Jesus Christ and he believed in three manifestations of one God rather than three persons of God. Paul said in I Timothy 3:16 God was manifested and was received back up into glory and John said in 1 John 1:1-2 Jesus Christ is a manifestation of one God and we have seen it. This understanding of the scriptures, by Paul and the apostles, is the same understanding and belief of the early Modalists, Sabellianists and Monarchianists. (John 1:1-14, Philippians 2:6, I John 1:1-2).

Three persons of one God is not in the Bible. The Trinitarian concept of who God is; is a heresy and is not true. (Matthew 15:7-9, II Timothy 3:16).

The discussions from historical Church councils about the oneness of God and the Person of Jesus Christ have caused a great falling away from the doctrine of Christ. The question is this. Is the Trinity a sound doctrine or a conspiracy?

"Jesus is Lord (Yeshua is Yahweh)"
(Gen. 17:1, Deut. 6:4, Isa. 9:6, 43:11, Luke 2:11,
John 1:10, 8:24, 58, Titus 2:13, Rev. 1:7-8)

CHAPTER 34

SOUND DOCTRINE

There is a conspiracy against sound doctrine. At the council of Constantinople 381AD, the Trinitarian doctrine was ratified and became a complicated doctrine of three persons in one God, thereby, making the doctrine of Jesus Christ unintelligible and a conspiracy against sound doctrine. In modern times saints are told you don't have to understand the Trinity; just believe it. That's ludicrous!!

We have found the Trinitarian doctrine is not a sound doctrine because it can't be explained, understood nor logically proven in scripture. All scripture that seems to point to three persons are "assumptions," not facts. Remember the paradigm shift. Facts can be proven by scripture, assumptions cannot be Biblically proven.

In addition, the Trinity is confusing and cannot be proven by most Christian writers. Karen Armstrong is just one example of a well known writer of Christian theology who is challenged to explain the Trinity and believes the Trinity is a manmade doctrine.

Karen Armstrong wrote in the introduction of her book, "A History of God, The 4,000-Year Quest of Judaism, Christianity and Islam" pg. xviii;

> "*Did the New Testament really teach the elaborate – and highly self contradictory – doctrine of the Trinity or was this, like so many*

other articles of faith, a fabrication by theologians centuries after the death of Christ in Jerusalem?"

I absolutely agree with Ms. Armstrong's confusion of a "three person" God and her assertion the Trinity is indeed a man made doctrine. There is no question the Trinity is a paganistic/polytheistic concept of who God is not. Since the Trinity cannot be proven in the Word of God, why would we want to teach a doctrine that is not in the Bible? (Galatians 1:8-9).

The Trinitarian doctrine is taught because Christian followers of Jesus Christ don't know Jesus Christ nor do they know the Father (John 14:6-7). When Jesus talks of his Father, he was speaking to his own Spirit in his body. He never called this Spirit another person in the Godhead. In other words, the Father (Spirit) is in the body of Jesus Christ and is in heaven at the same time. (John 14:6-12, Colossians 1:19, 2:8-12, I Timothy 3:16).

Followers of the Trinitarian doctrine will not endure sound doctrine. "For the time will come when they will not endure sound doctrine; but after their own lusts shall they heap to themselves teachers, having itching ears". God is so concerned about sound doctrine, it's mentioned on more than one occasion.

Sound doctrine is understandable and irrefragable.

The Trinity, a doctrine of men, can't be understood. Let's look at the base element of the Trinity and why it can't be understood; three persons = three gods. That's an unsound doctrine.

God did not deliver to the saints an unsound doctrine which is by all indications, the doctrine of the Trinity. The base element of the Trinity is one of the causes of debate in Christianity. Is God, one, two, or three? The sound Biblical doctrine is; God is one. Let's see what God thinks about an unsound doctrine which is called, historically, the Trinitarian Doctrine. According to Colossians 2:8-9, man will introduce traditions of men and deny the one Lord God who is in the body of Jesus Christ (Luke 2:11).

I **Timothy 1:10** For whoremongers, for them that defile themselves with mankind, for menstealers, for liars, for perjured persons, and if there be any other thing that is contrary to sound doctrine;

II Timothy 4:3 For the time will come when they will not endure sound doctrine; but after their own lusts shall they heap to themselves teachers, having itching ears;

Titus 1:9 Holding fast the faithful word as he hath been taught, that he may be able by sound doctrine both to exhort and to convince the gainsayers.

Titus 2:1 But speak thou the things which become sound doctrine:

This book explains the sound doctrine of the apostles and the doctrine of Jesus Christ. Christians should search for the truth of the apostles' doctrine for themselves (Acts 2:42, Titus 1:9, Titus 2:1).

The mystery of God's Word will only be revealed to believers who have a pure heart and those who are diligently searching for the truth of Jesus Christ and the oneness of God without their own preconceived ideas. While reading this book, your own heart will tell you whether you are a believer or non-believer in the Word of God. God's Word will grip your heart and you will either confess or not confess in your heart Jesus Christ is Lord, the one God of heaven and earth and not three persons. (Genesis 17:1, John 1:10, Revelation 1:7-8).

Kenneth E. Lamb wrote in the *"Pentecostal Herald,"*

> *"There is a new monotheistic movement Brewing". "It's drawing Trinitarian Christians out of the confusion of a "three God" theology.*

Christian writers and scholars have told us on many occasions the Trinity is a Christian theology, however, that theology cannot be logically understood nor Biblically explained. I like things simple and understandable. Thus, we know three in one God doesn't make sense except in a fraction and God is not a fraction. God is a whole; therefore, we can't say God is three (3) in one (1). Three in one as it relates to God doesn't make sense. God is one and he is Jesus Christ the Jewish Messiah

"Jesus is Lord (Yeshua is Yahweh)"
(Gen. 17:1, Deut. 6:4, Isa. 9:6, 43:11, Luke 2:11,
John 1:10, 8:24, 58, Titus 2:13, Rev. 1:7-8)

CHAPTER 35

JESUS CHRIST IS THE JEWISH MESSIAH

There is a conspiracy against Jesus Christ being the Jewish Messiah. The only way we can determine Jesus Christ is the Jewish Messiah is by studying the Old and New Testaments and putting the pieces together (revelation). There are many scriptures we can put together to prove Jesus Christ is the Jewish Messiah. God is a mystery who has revealed himself to the saints. (Reference; *"Understanding the Trinity, Three Persons vs Three Manifestations"*). Let's take a look at a few scriptures to prove Jesus Christ is the promised Messiah (God in Flesh). These scriptures are written out for two reasons;

1. For your convenience. If you don't have a Bible available, it will be easy to understand the scriptural references if we just write them out and put them together.
2. Jews and Muslims might not have a New Testament Bible readily available. However they do believe in the Old Testament: Deuteronomy 6:4 (Shema). "Hear, O Israel: The Lord our God is one Lord:

Based on Deuteronomy 6:4, there is no question God wants Israel to understand he is one Lord. Therefore, the Hebrews/Israelites/Jews can't believe in three persons in one God. The statement God is three persons is not consistent with the Old or the New Testament.

When God says One Lord; does not mean there are three persons in one Lord. God doesn't know any other god or persons in the Godhead other than himself. Why would anyone challenge the Word of God when God himself doesn't know any other persons in the Godhead other than himself? In order for Jews to get a clear picture of their Messiah, they must first understand the 53rd Chapter of Isaiah.

In Chapter 53:7, we find; "He was oppressed and he was afflicted, yet he opened not his mouth: he is brought as the lamb to the slaughter, and as a lamb to the slaughter, and as a sheep before her shearers is dumb, so he openeth not his mouth. (Jesus-Yeshua) in the New Testament: Acts 8:32-38.

Verse 8. He was taken from prison and from judgment: and who shall declare his generation? For he was cut off out of the land of the living: for the transgression of my people was he stricken. (Jesus-Yeshua) in the New Testament: Matthew 27:15-26.

Verse 10. Yet it pleased the Lord to bruise him; he hath put him to grief: when thou shalt make his soul an offering for sin, he shall see his seed, he shall prolong his days, and the pleasure of the Lord shall prosper in his hand. (Jesus-Yeshua) in the New Testament: Matthew 27:27-37.

Old Testament: Zechariah 12:10. And I will pour upon the house of David, and upon the inhabitants of Jerusalem, the spirit of grace and of supplications: and they shall look upon me whom they have pierced, and they shall mourn for him, as one mourneth for his only son, and shall be in bitterness for him, as one that is in bitterness for his firstborn (Jesus-Yeshua) in the New Testament: John 19:34, Revelation 1:7-8).

Comment: This proves the Jewish Messiah was crucified for the sins of mankind and his name is Jesus Christ, the Lamb of God. Jesus Christ is the name of the same Lord in Deuteronomy 6:4, in his form as the Spirit (Word) of God (John 1:14).

Now let's contrast the Old Testament scriptures with the New Testament so we can see Jesus satisfied all of the scriptures in the Old Testament to prove he is the Jewish Messiah in the New Testament.

New Testament: Luke 2:11

Verse 11. For unto you is born this day in the city of David a Saviour, which is Christ the Lord (Isaiah 9:6).

Comment: This scripture proves the one Lord in the Old Testament is the same Lord in the New Testament. There are not two Lords. God is Lord in his Spirit form and he is the same Lord in the Flesh as the Lord Jesus Christ (Deuteronomy 6:4, John 1:1-14, Colossians 1:19, 2:8-9).

New Testament: Matthew 1:23.

Verse 23. Behold a virgin shall be with child, and shall bring forth a son, and they shall call his name Emmanuel, which being interpreted is, God with us. (Isaiah 7:14, 8:8).

Comment: In this scripture, God is telling us Jesus Christ is the God with us. Seeing there is only one God, Jesus Christ is the one and only true God manifested in the flesh. (Isaiah 9:6, 43:10, John 14:6-9, I Corinthians 10:4, II Corinthians 5:19, I Timothy 3:16, I John 5:20, Titus 2:13, Jude 1:25).

New Testament: John 1:1, 3, 10, 11, 14

Verse 1. In the beginning was the Word, and the Word was with God, and the Word was God.

Comment: When God talks of himself as the Word, he lets us know Christ is God. When God speaks of the Word with him, he is telling us his voice and his mind which is with him is God. Thus, God is Christ in his Spirit form (Acts 9:5, I Corinthians 10:4).

God is not speaking to some other God or person in the Godhead. Jews never believed nor had an understanding God is speaking to some other God. Jews believe God is absolutely one in creation. (Deuteronomy 6:4, Isaiah 44:24, Colossians 2:8-12). Only Gentiles believe God is talking to someone else.

Verse 3. All things were made by him; and without him was not anything made that was made.

Comment: All things were made by Jesus Christ as the Word in his Spirit form (Colossians 1:14-19).

Verse 10. he was in the world, and the world was made by him, and the world knew him not.

Comment: God proves through John he made the world as Jesus Christ, the Word, and the world didn't know him when he walked on earth as a man. (Colossians 1:14-19).

Verse 11. He came unto his own, and his own received him not.

Comment: God who is Jesus Christ in the flesh came to his own chosen people and they wouldn't receive him (Matthew 1:23, II Corinthians 5:19).

Verse 14. And the word was made flesh, and dwelt among us, (and we beheld his glory, the glory as of the only begotten of the Father,) full of grace and truth.

Comment: God is Jesus Christ who is the Word and the one and only true God made flesh (Luke 2:11, I John 1:1-2, 5:20, Titus 2:13, Jude 1:25, Revelation 1:7-8)

Comment: These verses prove again God revealed himself by putting his Spirit into flesh. Jesus Christ as the Word in his Spiritual form, revealed himself as Jesus Christ so we would be able to see his glory (John 14:6-9, I Corinthians 10:4, Hebrews 1:3, Colossians 2:8-9, I John 1:1-2).

New Testament: John 4:25-26.

Verse 25. The woman saith unto him, I know that Messias cometh, which is called Christ: when he is come, he will tell us all things.

Verse 26. Jesus saith unto her, I that speak unto thee am he. (Isaiah 43:10-11)

Comment: This scripture couldn't be any plainer for the Jews. Jesus Christ himself has declared he is the Messiah and his words can be proven throughout both the Old and New Testaments.

New Testament: John 19:33-37

Verse 33. But when they came to Jesus, and saw that he was dead already, they brake not his legs:

Verse 34. But one of the soldiers with a spear pierced his side, and forthwith came out blood and water (Zechariah 12:10).

Verse 35. And he that saw it bare record, and his record is true: and he knoweth that he saith true, that ye might believe.

Verse 36. For these things were done, that the scripture should be fulfilled, A bone of him shall not be broken.

Verse 37. And again another scripture saith, They shall look on him whom they pierced (Zechariah 12:10).

Comment: Based on these scriptures, Jesus Christ is the Messiah as foretold by John 19:36-37 which says a bone of him shall not be broken. In addition, in Zechariah 12:10, Jesus Christ is the Messiah, the Son of God, whom they, the Roman soldiers, pierced. Jesus Christ is the Almighty God who was pierced (Revelation 1:7-8).

New Testament: Revelation 1:7-8

Verse 7. Behold, he cometh with clouds; and every eye shall see him, and they also which pierced him: and all kindreds of the earth shall wail because of him. Even so, Amen.

Verse 8. I am Alpha and Omega, the beginning and the ending, saith the Lord, which is, and which was, and which is to come, the Almighty.

There is no question Jesus Christ is Lord, and the oneness of God is true. In conclusion, the time has come to bring all of God's Christian saints together under a new revolutionary oneness Christian theology because the oneness of God is truth. (Deuteronomy 6:4, Luke 2:11, Acts 10:36).

"Jesus is Lord (Yeshua is Yahweh)"
(Gen. 17:1, Deut. 6:4, Isa. 9:6, 43:11, Luke 2:11,
John 1:10, 8:24, 58, Titus 2:13, Rev. 1:7 8)

CHAPTER 36

THE ONENESS OF GOD IS TRUTH

The two major mysteries God stressed to his prophets and the "people of the book" were the power of his name and the oneness of his nature is true. The following facts can be researched in the Bible and the Public Library, and will give you an understanding of how many times, and in how many ways God has proven his oneness. Let's take a look at the following encounters wherein God told His prophets about the power of his name and the oneness of his nature.

1. **Abraham, Isaac, Jacob, Ishmael, and the Prophets.** Hebrews/ Israelites/Jews would have been called, historically, Modalists/ Sabellianists who believe in numerous manifestations of one God (Exodus 3:4, 13:21, Daniel 3:25, Hebrews 1:1).

   God manifested himself to the prophets in various ways and in various forms or manifestations as one God. (Exodus 3:14, John 8:58, Hebrews 1:3). God never spoke of himself as a "three person" Trinity. God spoke of the power of his name and the oneness of his nature to the Old Testament prophets. They worshipped God on Saturday (Sabbath).

2. **Paul and the Apostles (the first apostolic Christians)** would have been called, historically, Modalists/Sabellianists who believe in

the three manifestations of one God for the salvation of mankind (John 1:1-14, 14:17, I Timothy 3:16, I John 1:1).

Paul and the apostles knew nothing about a Trinity and never preached nor taught it; they were dead long before the adoption of the Trinity in 325AD. (Galatians 1:6-9). God spoke of the power of his name and the oneness of his nature to Paul and the apostles. (I Corinthians 10:4, Acts 4:12). They worshipped God on Saturday and Sunday. They baptized new converts in the name of Jesus Christ (Matthew 28:19, Acts 2:38, 4:12, 19:1-5, Colossians 2:8-12).

3. **Gentile Trinitarian Christians** made a distortion of God's Word, His oneness, and His name by introducing a doctrine of men called the Trinity beginning at the Nicene Council 325AD (Colossians 2:8). This council was and is a satanic conspiracy against the oneness of God and against Jesus Christ and the Christian Church. They baptize new converts in God's titles; the Father, the Son, and the Holy Ghost (Matthew 28:19).

4. **Oneness Pentecostal Christians**. God is bringing Christians back to the oneness of His nature through the modern day Oneness Apostolic Pentecostal Christians. The original Oneness Pentecostal Christians, Peter, James, John, and the apostle Paul believed in the three manifestations (forms) of one God (the Father, Son, and Holy Ghost as manifestations of one God) for the salvation of mankind (John 1:1-14, 14:17, I Timothy 3:16, I John 1:1-2).

The original Oneness Apostolic Pentecostal Christians (the apostles) worshipped God on Saturday and Sunday. For most Christians, the first day of the week (Sunday) is a day of celebration because the resurrection was on the first day of the week.

Today, God is once again bringing the power of his name and the Oneness of his nature to the world through the mystery, revelation, and knowledge of the apostles' doctrine through the Jewish Apostolic Christians and the Oneness Apostolic Pentecostal Christians. (Acts 2:42).

Based on all my research and study of the major religions, I have found the apostles' doctrine followed by the Oneness Apostolic Pentecostal Christians is the original gospel of Jesus Christ and the revelation of the power of God's name and the oneness of his nature as preached by the prophets, and the apostles (Deuteronomy 6:4, Isaiah 45:23, Philippians 2:11).

The scriptures in this book verify the power of God's name and the oneness of his nature. Jesus Christ is the Father, Son, and Holy Ghost who is also the one Lord God Almighty and the rock (name) upon which the Church is built by baptism in the name of Jesus Christ and the gates of hell shall not prevail against it. "For who is God, save the LORD? and who is a rock, save our God?" (II Samuel 22:32, Ps 18:31, I Corinthians 10:4).

Jesus Christ, by his own admission, is the Almighty God and he is the God (rock) who was pierced and died for the sins of mankind by shedding his own blood (Zechariah 12:10, Acts 20:28, John 1:10, Revelation 1:7-8).

Thus this same Jesus Christ is our One Lord, God, Saviour, Christ, and Messiah of the "People of the Book". God is very clear concerning the power of his name and the oneness of His nature. Keeping this in mind, Oneness Apostolic Christians baptize new converts in the name of Jesus Christ (Matthew 28:19, Acts 2:38, 4:12, 19:1-5, Colossians 2:8-12).

5. **Islam and the Prophet Muhammad.** The Prophet Muhammad was born in 570AD well after the Council of Nicaea in 325AD. God proclaimed his oneness again through the Prophet Muhammad. And according to the Muslims God spoke, through Gabriel, to Muhammad and told him to proclaim the power of his name and the oneness of his nature to the world. God forbade Muhammad to talk about him as a Trinity. (Surah 5:73).

In summary, based on what we have learned through our understanding of scripture; we can conclude God wants to bring us back to a new revolutionary oneness Christian theology by giving us an understanding of the oneness of God, an understanding of the conspiracy against Jesus Christ and the Christian Church, an understanding of the keys of the kingdom of heaven, an understanding of the "great commission", an understanding of the apostles doctrine, anunderstanding of how salvation is built upon a rock by the baptism in Jesus name, an understanding on how to be born again, and by giving us an understanding of the power of His name in the face of Jesus Christ, a manifestation of God Himself. Based on our understanding of the oneness of God and the differences in all faiths and religions, we must search for a purer form of Christianity so we can all speak the same things that were suggested by the apostle Paul in I Corinthians. Therefore we would like to introduce a name for a new revolutionary "oneness" Christian Church.

"Jesus is Lord (Yeshua is Yahweh)"
(Gen. 17:1, Deut. 6:4, Isa. 9:6, 43:11, Luke 2:11,
John 1:10, 8:24, 58, Titus 2:13, Rev. 1:7-8)

CHAPTER 37

A NEW REVOLUTIONARY "ONENESS" CHRISTIAN THEOLOGY

There has been a concerted effort by Satan to cause confusion in Christian theology about the Trinity and the Oneness of God. In today's world we see a doctrine which is not believable, not consistent, and not cohesive. Christians, as a whole, refuse to teach a sound doctrine. Our doctrines are so different from what the apostles taught, it seems, we will never agree. Therefore, we must return to a new/old revolutionary oneness Christian theology of the apostles (Apostles Doctrine), a purer form of Christianity.

As Christians, we belong to some type of denomination which has its own doctrine, even if you belong to a non-denomination Church. Non-Denomination is a denomination. Through study we find there are no denominations mentioned in the Bible. There is only one God, one gospel, one salvation, and one Lord Jesus Christ.

Therefore, we should seek Biblical Church doctrine. If we want to know what Christians should be called and what denomination we should seek; we should use only Biblical names and terms so as not to cause confusion. I'm not advocating you leave your preferred church denomination. The purpose of this analogy is to find a level of Christian agreement that will bring us all back into the knowledge and the truth of the oneness of God and the Torah (God's teaching and instruction).

I have a friend who said, there is no way you are going to get Christians to agree on anything. I hope to prove him wrong. Paul said, in 1 Corinthians 1:10, 13-15. Now I beseech you, brethren, by the name of our Lord Jesus Christ, that ye all speak the same thing and that there be no divisions among you, but that ye be perfectly joined together in the same mind and in the same judgment. (The Trinitarian doctrine of 325AD is not the same mind)

Verse 13. Is Christ divided? Was Paul crucified for you? Or were ye baptized in the name of Paul?

Verse 14. I thank God that I baptized none of you, but Crispus and Gaius,

Verse 15. Lest any should say that I had baptized in mine own name.

Paul was talking about baptism. Baptism was performed in a name and not God's titles mentioned in Matthew 28:19. The name Paul was referring to is revealed in Acts 2:38, 8:16, 10:48, 22:16, and 19:1-5. Paul was speaking about understanding the same thing concerning baptism in a name. Realizing that baptism was performed in no other name, for we are bought with a price through the blood of Christ. The name of Jesus Christ is the only name which carries the blood that washes our sins away. The name Jesus Christ and the blood are inseparable. (Matthew 28:19-in the name, Acts 2:38-the keys of the kingdom-baptism in the name of Jesus Christ, Colossians 2:9, in the body of, Acts 4:12-no other name).

According to Paul, God want all Christians (Jews and Gentiles) to speak the same thing concerning the oneness of God, baptism, and salvation. In my heart, I could feel the Lord showing me a new revolutionary way to explain the oneness of God from a Christian standpoint.

After meditating for months, I could see how this new revolutionary oneness Christian Church should be called, SOAPICC, "washing away the Ignorance and Confusion of Christianity".

195

I had an uncomfortable feeling about even talking about a new name for a Christian Church until I heard a sermon by Sister Mary Kloepper about having "gumption". I had to rethink my ideas about SOAPICC. I was compelled to continue in my understanding of this new revolutionary oneness understanding of Christianity. Let me give you some history.

On many occasions over the years, God has spoken to me through my Pastor Michael Williams, a dynamic preacher and a powerful man of God, at the Pentecostals of Apopka. Pastor Williams' sermons have dramatically changed my life and my relationship with Jesus Christ, the one Lord God of heaven and earth. At times, being led by the Holy Spirit, Pastor Williams would use the talents of the pulpit staff to bring the message.

On January 18, 2012, Sister Mary Kloepper, a powerful woman of God, a pianist, an artist (oil painting), a recording artist, teacher, speaker, and a member of The Pentecostals preached. Sister Kloepper preached a sermon called, "It's Time to Get out of the Boat". (Reference: Gumption)

This message had a profound effect on my life and the direction God was leading me because I had been thinking about SOAPICC. I had to get out of the boat and raise awareness that Christians should speak the same things about the oneness of God, the Deity of Jesus Christ, the method of salvation, baptism, and the reception of the Holy Spirit. She talked about an old southern term called, "gumption".

When one is able to have the initiative and enterprise to step out of the ordinary and do something extraordinary that's gumption. She suggested Peter certainly possessed a lot of good old fashioned gumption. Peter didn't want to be sitting in the boat when something this big was about to take place. He wanted to be part of something greater than he could even begin to imagine.

She said; how many of us sitting here tonight have enough gumption to do the unusual, the unpredictable. What is your boat? Your boat is whatever you choose in which to place your trust. Peter didn't think about sinking or failure when he stepped out of the boat.

She expressed we should step out of the norm and follow God's prompting in our life. We must step out of the ordinary to experience the extraordinary. God will move us out of our personal or perceived limitations.

All I could see, as Sis. Kloepper suggested, was all the obstacles I had to overcome, the setbacks and hazards I had to endure. I didn't want to take a spiritual risk. I was out of my comfort zone. She said, obedience doesn't mean I'm not going to have adversity; I must be willing to step out of the boat. There is no guarantee life in the boat is going to be any safer. What an amazing word coming through this great woman of God on my behalf. God was speaking directly to me. I was afraid I would be misunderstood and ostracized because of what God was prompting me to do. In my mind, SOAPICC was a concept that was too radical.

God had lain on my heart I should go forth with what He was prompting me to do. Now, I realized, based on Sis. Kloepper's sermon; God wanted me to get out of the boat and do what He was prompting me to do. God was prompting me to write on a new revolutionary name for a Oneness Christian Church. This new revolutionary oneness Church involved the necessity of communication among Christians of all faiths concerning salvation and the gospel of Jesus Christ (I Corinthians 1:10-15).

How do we change our thoughts about Christianity and how do we get this new revolutionary Christian Church to the world? We have to start by going back to the scriptures to get a better understanding of the beginning of the original Christian faith, a purer form of Christianity. Let's take a look at the meaning of each concept to come to the whole of this old/new "oneness" theology of Christianity. It's time to step out of the boat and create a new Oneness Christian Church which could be called, SOAPICC, washing away the ignorance and confusion of Christianity (a purer form of Christianity - the apostles doctrine)..

"Jesus is Lord (Yeshua is Yahweh)"
(Gen. 17:1, Deut. 6:4, Isa. 9:6, 43:11, Luke 2:11,
John 1:10, 8:24, 58, Titus 2:13, Rev. 1:7-8)

Chapter 38

SOAPICC and the
Oneness of God

(A purer form of Christianity)

Washing away the ignorance and Confusion of Christianity

Christian Churches should be called, Sabbath/Sunday Oneness Apostolic Pentecostal International Christian Church (SOAPICC)–translated: "washing away the Ignorance and Confusion of Christianity". Now, let's take a closer look at the meaning of SOAPICC;

SOAP	**"washing away"** (A paganistic/polytheistic doctrine of the Trinity)
	The
International	**"Ignorance"** (How to be born again, using John 3:5, Matt 28:19 and Acts 2:38)
	And
Christian	**"Confusion"** (God is one Person not "three persons– Job 13:6-11, Heb. 1:3, 8)
	Of
Church	**Christianity"** (Salvation: Keys of the kingdom– Matthew 16:18-19, Act 2:38)

The following concepts will bring believers back to the Deity of Jesus Christ and the oneness of His nature. We must come back to the original practices and doctrine of the apostles (Acts 2:42).

Sabbath Day (under the Law (Torah) and Sunday after the resurrection (under Grace)

God has always admonished the Israelites they should remember the Sabbath and keep it holy under the Law (Torah – God's teaching and instruction) of Moses. The original Christian apostles worshipped God on the Sabbath (Saturday) and on the first day of the week (Sunday). When and why did we change God's holy day from Saturday (Sabbath) to Sunday?

According to church history starting at the Nicene Council 325, the Sabbath Day was changed by the Bishops at the Ecumenical Council of Churches from Saturday to Sunday. This decree was to be followed by all Christian Churches worldwide. These bishops could justify the change to Sunday based on the actions of the apostles who worshipped God on the first day of the week (Sunday) after the resurrection.

However, the real reason for the change to Sunday, was made to appease Constantine, a pagan, who wanted to worship the Sun God on Sunday. In addition, to pleasing Constantine, the bishops could also assure Christians they too were following the scriptures based on the actions of the apostles, on the first day of the week (Sunday).

Therefore, the bishops could say the change to Sunday is scriptural and can be proven. Let's take a look at the agreements and justifications used to change the day of worship to Sunday;

Saturday **Sabbath Day Worship** Matthew 12:8-9. (Jesus is Lord of the sabbath day)

Acts 13:14 (they went into the synagogue on the sabbath day)

Acts 15:21 (read in the synagogue every sabbath day)

Acts 16:13 (prayer was needed on the sabbath day)

Acts 17:2 (Paul reasoned with them on the sabbath day)

Acts 18:4 (Paul reasoned in the synagogue every sabbath)

Sunday Worship (1st day of the week) (Jesus arose at the end of the Sabbath and he was seen on the first day of the week–Sunday)

Matthew 28:1 (Jesus has arisen- this is a day of celebration of the newness of life)

Mark 16:2, 9 (Jesus has arisen- this is a day of celebration of the newness of life)

Luke 24:1 (Jesus has arisen- this is a day of celebration of the newness of life)

John 20:1, 19 (Jesus has arisen- this is a day of celebration of the newness of life)

Acts 2:46 (Every Day–on one accord in the temple)

Acts 20:7 (Paul preached on the first day of the week)

Romans 14:5 (don't judge; be persuaded in your own mind)

Romans 14:5-6 (whatever the day; regard it unto the Lord)

I Corinthians 16:1-2 (take up collection on the first day of the week)

Colossians 2:16-17 (let no man Judge you of the sabbath days)

Let's agree there are no evil days in God. I don't think Christians are in violation of scripture if we worship God on Sunday because Jesus Christ is the Lord of the Sabbath. He arose on Sunday (the 1st day of the week), a holy day of celebration for most Christians worldwide. After the resurrection, according to Acts 2:1- 42, the Sabbath was placed in our hearts, not by the will of man but by the grace of God. The incarnate Torah (Jesus Christ who is Lord of the Sabbath) was placed in our hearts.

Like circumcision, the Sabbath is a matter of the heart according to the renewed covenant (New Testament). The Sabbath is not one day any more. The Sabbath is every day because it is a matter of the heart. Christians can choose any day to celebrate Sabbath. Based on the Renewed Covenant, we can now say, "Remember your heart and keep it holy". Don't worry so much about the day; guard your heart. According to the renewed covenant the Sabbath is a matter of the heart not an activity by men who are seeking salvation by works. (Romans 14:5, Jeremiah 31:31-33, Hebrews 8:8-10).

We could return to our early practices and traditions of worshipping God on Saturday (the Sabbath) seeing that God asks us to keep the Sabbath holy under the Law (Torah – God's teaching and instruction).

We could keep the Sabbath (Saturday) and still be under the grace of Jesus Christ in the New Testament; seeing that the Law (Torah) is fulfilled in Jesus Christ, the incarnate Torah. The Sabbath is brought to a better understanding in the renewed covenant (New Testament). (Colossians 2:16-17).

We should judge no man concerning the Sabbath. Why? The Sabbath has been fulfilled in Jesus Christ. **We are no longer under the Law.** We are now under grace. (Romans 6:14-15). The Sabbath was made for man not man for the Sabbath. (Mark 2:27).

Study the Sabbath Day in the chapter on The Seventh Day Adventists. I believe, based on scripture, and the reception of the Holy Ghost, the Sabbath can be worshipped on any day we choose. We could for the sake of tradition revert back to worshipping God on the Sabbath (Saturday) if we choose; realizing that worshipping God on Sunday is not a violation of scripture. (Romans 14:1-5).

** **No longer under the Law - Insight**** From a Hebraic perspective, we are no longer under the Law means "we are no longer under the law of sin and death". In Hebrew the Law (Torah – God's teaching and instruction) is the foundation of our Christian faith and the Torah has been revealed and brought to a better understanding in Jesus Christ (a Renewed Covenant). Therefore, when we receive Christ, we receive the Torah and the Sabbath in our hearts. (Jeremiah 31:31-33, Hebrews 8:8-10).

Oneness Genesis 17:1, Rev. 1:8, Deut. 6:4, Luke 2:11, John 10:30 and Colossians 2:9 identifies Jesus Christ as the one Lord God Almighty.

Apostolic (Acts 2:42) The term "apostolic" comes from the apostles' doctrine mentioned in Acts 2:42. The apostles' doctrine is explained in this book and in my first book, "Understanding" The Trinity, three persons vs Three Manifestations.

To give a short answer, the apostles believed in the absolute oneness of God as manifested in the body of Jesus Christ, the baptism in Jesus name, and the reception of the Holy Ghost according to Matthew 28:19, Acts 2:38, 8:16, 10:48, 22:16, 19:1-5, Romans 6:3-4, Colossians 2:9-12, and Galatians 1:8-9. The Apostolic Church history is in the book of Acts (actions of the apostles).

Pentecostal (Acts 1: 1-43). The day of Pentecost is the day Jesus wanted the apostles to wait until they received power from on high. Jesus told Peter in Matthew 16:19, He would give him the keys of the kingdom of heaven. Peter used the keys on the day of Pentecost to open the door to Jesus Christ (the Church). We should all follow Peter's instructions because he received his directions directly from the Lord himself (Matthew 28:19, Acts 2:38). **The keys** (Torah – 613 Principles) of the kingdom of heaven are in Acts 2:38

Key #1. Repent to God-(**Name – Jesus Christ**)

Key #2. Be baptized in the name of Jesus Christ (incarnate Torah – Colossians 2:9 – Father, Son, and Holy Ghost) Matthew 16:18-19 (built upon a rock, I Corinthians. 10:4 – that rock was Christ), Matthew 28:19 (**Name – Jesus Christ**)

Key#3. Receive the gift of the Holy Ghost (**Name-Jesus Christ**) (Matthew 28:19, Jeremiah 31:31-33, Hebrews 8:8-10).

International - Matthew 28:19. This term is used because Jesus directed us to go into all the world and preach the gospel. Jesus' instructions concerning the gospel were consummated in Acts 2:38.

Christian - The apostles were called Christians because they were followers of Jesus Christ. Today, we should be called Christians, as well, because we are followers of Jesus Christ.

Church – The church is in the hearts of Christians as a manifestation of the Holy Spirit. At times the apostles used a physical place which were the homes of the saints. These gatherings were originally called the Church. Saints were given the opportunity to collectively serve our Lord and Saviour Jesus Christ in one location (Church – not as a matter of the heart but as a location).

I'm not concerned about what people call themselves as long as their names take on the tenants of Christianity. All Christian denominations should call themselves SOAPICC; Baptists, Seventh Day Adventists, Methodists, Pentecostal Assemblies of the World, Presbyterian, United Pentecostal Church, Unitarian Church, Messianic Judaism, Church of the Brethren, Church of God in Christ, Church of the Latter Day Saints, Church of the Nazarene, etc. It doesn't matter what your denomination is called, we can all speak the same thing as Paul suggests in I Corinthians 1:10-15. We should all wash away the ignorance and confusion of Christianity.

This is not a one world church theology. This is a coming together of those Oneness Apostolic Pentecostal Christian Churches, which believes in the Shema, the absolute oneness of God. Oneness Apostolic Pentecostal Christian Churches do not include tenants of Islam, the Catholic Church, nor the Trinity or Trinitarian Doctrine. (Research: the great deception of Islam, Catholicism, and the history of paganism in the Christian Church).

Oneness Apostolic Pentecostal Christianity is a standalone theology which believes in the Shema and the absolute oneness of God without the diabolical tenets from the council of Nicaea in 325AD, The Pope, the Catholic Church, Islam, and the new world order.

The dangers of Christianity come when we align ourselves with pagan religions which do not adhere to the doctrine of Jesus Christ nor the Shema. In these last days, we, oneness Christians (the nations – Ephraim - Israel) and Jews (Judah) must come together to witness the glorious appearing of our great God and Saviour Jesus Christ. There is going to be a great deception in those Trinitarian Churches who don't have a strong understanding of the oneness of God, the Deity of Jesus Christ, salvation, and the born again experience (Colossians 2:8-12, II Thessalonians 1:7-8, Titus 2:13, Revelation 1:7-8, Matthew 28:;19, Acts 2:38, Acts 4:12).

Finally, what is a purer form of Christianity;

1. A thorough understanding of the Shema (Deuteronomy 6:4, Luke 2:11, John 10:30).
2. A thorough understanding of the Deity of Jesus Christ (Isaiah 9:6, John 10:30-33, 14:1-12, Revelation 1:7-8).
3. A thorough understanding of the Apostolic doctrine and Church history (Acts 2:42)
4. A thorough understanding of the Trinitarian doctrine and Church history (Galatians 1:8-9).
5. A thorough understanding of the Sabbath Day as it relates to the New Testament (the Renewed Covenant - Jeremiah 31:31-33, Hebrew 8:8-10).
6. A thorough understanding of Apostolic Christianity (i.e. the apostles) as it relates to the Passover, the Tabernacle, Feast days, etc.
7. A thorough understanding of the Torah/the Tanakh (Old Testament) and its relationship with the New Testament (Renewed Covenant).
8. True Christianity does not include the celebration of pagan holidays such as;
    a. Christmas is a pagan holiday infused into Christianity by the Ecumenical Council 325 - 381AD). Christmas is a mixture of Christianity and a paganistic mass which uses idolatry as it's foundation (i.e. Christmas trees, Nativity dolls,

jingle bells, Santa Claus, and statues of the virgin Mary as the mother of God). Christmas (Christ – mass) was added to Christianity to appease Constantine and his fellow pagans who worshipped their various gods including Constantine's sun god on December 25.

b.   Easter is a pagan holiday infused into Christianity by the Ecumenical Council of Churches. Easter is a celebration of Constantine's pagan goddess Ishtar.

c.   Halloween is a paganistic celebration of evil. If the United States is a Christian nation, why would a Christian nation celebrate evil? Why would we recognize Halloween as a National holiday? We are horrified by evil, yet we celebrate Satan and evil once a year in these United States, that's idiotic. Why would we be sucked into a satanic system and build an economic system around evil?

d.   Mothers and Fathers Day celebrated in Churches gives praise and worship to man not to God (This is a tradition of men which is not a part of Jewish tradition).

e.   Pastor's Appreciation Day celebrated in Churches gives praise to man and not to God (this is not part of the apostolic doctrine).

9.   A thorough understanding of how to be born again (John 3:5, Matthew 28:19, Acts 2:38, 4:12, Romans 10:1-9, Colossians 2:8-12).
10. A thorough understanding of the keys (613 Principles of God) of the kingdom of heaven. Who gave the keys to whom, what were the keys, when were they used, what did they open, what did the keys have to do with salvation, what is the relationship between the keys and the born again experience, and what is the relationship between the keys and the "great commission"? (Matthew 16:18-19, Matthew 28:19, Acts 2:38).

After looking at all of the different religions and theologies, we have to ask ourselves what is the scriptural plum line? The scriptural plum line is the Word of God which is revealed in the Apostles Doctrine.

If the Apostles didn't do any paganistic holidays in the New Testament Church, why should we do these traditional paganistic activities in the Church today? Let's go back to our Christian roots which are based on the Torah (God's teaching and instructions) and get a better understanding of the dictates of God. Without the basic understanding of the oneness of God (Shema) and the Torah, one will never completely understand salvation, the born again experience, nor the Deity of Jesus Christ. Rabbi Messer said it best in the conclusion.

"Jesus is Lord (Yeshua is Yahweh)"
(Gen. 17:1, Deut. 6:4, Isa. 9:6, 43:11, Luke 2:11,
John 1:10, 8:24, 58, Titus 2:13, Rev. 1:7-8)

CHAPTER 39

CONCLUSION

Rabbi Ralph Messer writes in his book, TORAH: LAW OR GRACE? Kingdom PRINCIPLES for Kingdom LIVING.

> *"Therefore, if the God of Abraham, Isaac, and Jacob is the God of the Tanakh, and "God is One" (Shema), then the God of the New Testament must be the same God! Why then does Christianity often appear to be introducing a "new" Jesus, "new" commands and a "replacing/new" Covenant which is distinctly inconsistent and even contrary to earlier Biblical Principles? The truth is He is NOT a "new" Jesus! He IS the Word of YHWH "made flesh" Who appeared to Abraham in Genesis 15..............He IS the Salvation of the Living God (Isaiah 12), the visible Manifestation of the invisible God (Colossians 1:15), and the very fullness of YHWH God's indwelling bodily (Colossians 2:9). Therefore we conclude... Yeshua IS YHWH!*

> *..........Scripturally, whatever natural explanation or illustration you choose to use to describe the Incarnation of God as Yeshua/ Jesus, you cannot nullify the foundational Truth that "God is One, and there is no other!" The strongest opposition that Yeshua faced from the religious leaders of His day was not against His miracle-working, power or His inspired teaching of the Torah. The clear message of the Gospel-the "God News"-is that Jesus IS YHWH,*

and YHWH desires to dwell with and within His people by the Power of the Holy Spirit!

Jesus in His Divinity is YHWH...

and in His humanity is Man.

Jesus in His Divinity is the Father...

and in his humanity is the Son.

Jesus in His Divinity is Spirit...

and in His humanity is Flesh.

Jesus in His Divinity came to save us

and in His humanity He died to redeem us. Ibid, pg. 58-59(c) 2011.

In the final analysis, we are drawn to the fact that the Bible explains the absolute oneness of God and the power of his name. When we take everything in consideration, and all of the religions mentioned, we would have to conclude that Ephesians 4:5 has been proven. There really is **one Lord** (Deuteronomy 6:4, Luke 2:11, Acts 10:36), **one Faith** (Acts 2:42) **and one Baptism** (Acts 2:38, John 19:1-5, Colossians 3:17, I Peter 3:21).

We should all follow the apostles' doctrine so we can understand repentance, baptism in Jesus name, receiving the gift of the Holy Ghost, and understanding the oneness of God in the face of our Lord and Saviour Jesus Christ, who is the Father, the Son, and the Holy Ghost (Colossians 2:8-12). Thus, we can understand the oneness of God and the conspiracy against Jesus Christ and the Christian Church. Finally, **what is the conspiracy**?

"The Trinity of Three Persons" in one God is

****The Conspiracy against Jesus Christ****

and

****The Christian Church****

Now, permit me to introduce you to;

Our One Lord God Almighty

And

Our Saviour

"Jesus Christ"

Yeshua HaMashiach

(*Yahweh*)

(Gen. 17:1, Deut. 6:4, Isa. 9:6, 43:11, Luke 2:11, John 1:10, 14, 8:24, 58, Titus 2:13, Jude 1:25, Rev. 1:7-8)

BIBLIOGRAPHY

Arendzen, J. P. "Understanding the Trinity," Sophia Institute Press, Manchester, New Hampshire, Copy right 2004.

Armstrong, Karen, "A History of God," Ballantine Book, copy right 1993, Div of Random House.

Baillie, D.M. "God was in Christ". London: Faber and Faber Ltd, copyright 1947.

Bainton, Roland. "Early Christianity" Princeton, N.J. D. Van Nostrand Co. copyright 1960.

Barnes, A. Barnes, Notes on Old & New Testament, Baker Book House, copyright 1979.

Beasley-Murray, G.R. "Baptism in the New Testament," Grand Rapids: Eerdmans Publishing Company, copyright 1994.

Berkhof, Louis, "The History of Christian Doctrines," Grand Rapids, Baker Books, copyright, 1937.

Bernard, D.K. "The New Birth". Word Aflame Press, 8855 Dunn Road, Hazelwood, Mo 63042, copyright, 1984.

Bernard, D.K. "The Oneness of God". U.S.A. Word Aflame Press, 8855 Dunn Road, Hazelwood, Mo 63042, copyright, 1983-2000.

Bernard, D. K. "Oneness and Trinity" A.D. 100-300, Word Aflame Press, 8855 Dun Road, Hazelwood, Mo. 63042, copyright, 1992.

Bloom, Jonathan and Sheila Blair, "Islam, A Thousand Years of Faith and Power". Yale University Press, New Haven and London, First published as a Yale Nota Bene book in 2002, originally published in 2000 by Gardner Films, copyright by Jonathan Bloom and Sheila Blair in 2002.

Burgess, S.M. and McGee, G. Dictionary of Pentecostal and Charismatic Movements. Grand Rapids, Zondervan, copyright 1988.

Chalfant, W. "Ancient Champions of Oneness," A History of the True Church of Jesus Christ U.S.A, Word Aflame Press, copyright 1982.

Daniels, Will, "Understanding the Trinity, three persons vs Three Manifestations, Authorhouse Publishing, copyright 2009.

Jones, Eddie, "The Truth About One God," Newspaper, Bud Tingle, Madison, Ky, copyright July 1998.

Erickson, Millard J. "Making Sense of the Trinity, Three Crucial Questions," Baker Academic, copyright 2000.

Esposito, John L. "What Everyone Needs to Know About Islam," Oxford University Press Inc., 198 Madison Avenue, New York, New York, 10016, copyright 2002.

Fish III, John H, edited, "Understanding the Trinity" ECS Ministries, P.O. Box 1028, Dubuque, IA 52004-1028, copyright 2006.

Grumbine, G.C.F., "The Secret Doctrine of The Order of Melchizedek in the Bible," published by Research Associates School Times Publication 751 East 75th Street, Chicago, Il 60619. And Miguel Lorne Publishers, Jamaica, P.O. Box 2967, Kingston 8, Jamaica. Copyright 1919, 2003.

Goldstein, Don, "I Have a Friend Who's Jewish Do You? Shivat Tzion Ministries copyright February 25, 2004.

Gonzalez, Justo. "A History of Christian Thought". Nashville: Abingdon, copy right 1975.

Graves, R. B. "The God of Two Testaments, U.S.A: Robert Graves and James Turner, copyright 1977.

Hastings, James, ed. "Encyclopedia of Religion and Ethics". New York, Charles Scribner's Sons, copyright 1951.

Haywood, G. T. "The Birth of the Spirit," Christ Temple, 430 W. Fall Creek Pkwy Indianapolis. Ind. (317) 923-7278

Kelly, J.N.D. "Early Christian Doctrine". 5th, ed. London: Adam & Charles Black, copyright 1980.

Klotsche, E. H. "The History of Christian Doctrine". Rev. ed. Grand Rapids, Baker, copyright 1945, 1979.

Kuhn, Thomas "The Structure of Scientific Revolution," University of Chicago Press, copyright 1962.

Lamb, Kenneth E. "There is a New Monotheistic Movement Brewing," Pentecostal Herald, Sec. World News, 8855 Dunn Road, Hazelwood, Mo. 63042, copyright Aug. 1997

Latourette, Kenneth Scott, "A History of Christianity". Rev. ed. San Francisco, Harper and Row, copyright 1953, 1975..

Lightfoot, J.B. and Hermer, J.R. :The Apostolic Fathers, 2nd ed. Leicester: Apollos, 1989.

Lippman, Thomas W. "Understanding ISLAM" An Introduction To The Muslim World, Second Revised Edition, A Meridan Book, Published by the Penguin Group, copyright 1982, 1990, 1995.

McGrath, Alistler E. "Understanding the Trinity," Academic Book is an imprint of Zondervan Publishing House, 1415 Lake Drive, S. E., Grand Rapids, Michigan 49506, copyright 1988, 1990.

Ministerial Association, "Seventh-day Adventists Believe........A Biblical Exposition of 27 Fundamental Doctrines," General Conference of Seventh-day Advents, 6840 Eastern Avenue NW. Washington, D.C. 20012, copyright 1988.

Orlando Sentinel, 633 N. Orange Ave. Orlando, Fla. A Tribune Publishing Company, 435 North Michigan Ave, Chicago, IL., 60611.

Pacific Institute, "When the United States Passes the National Sunday Law" as Predicted in the Bible, P.O. Box 33111, San Diego, Ca 92163, copyright 1996.

Peterson, J. "The Real Truth About Baptism in Jesus Name" . U.S.A. Pentecostal Publishing House, copyright 1953.

Pugh, J. T. "How to Receive the Holy Ghost," Hazelwood, Mo. Pentecostal Publishing House, copyright 1969.

Rabbi Ralph Messer. The TORAH: LAW OR GRACE? Kingdom PRINCIPLES for Kingdom LIVING Simchat Torah Beit Midrash Publishing, P.O. Box 4810, Parker, Colorado, 80134, Copyright 2011, Rabbi Ralph Messer.

Rambsel, Yacov A. "His Name is Jesus," Toronto, Ontario, Canada, copyright 1997, 1999.

Roy E. Graham, "Ellen G. White," Co-founder of the Seventh-day Church, American University Studies, Series VII Theology and Religion, Vol. 12., Peter Lang, New York, Berne, Frankfurt am Main.

Seventh – Day Adventist, "Elder's Handbook, Baptism," The Ministerial Association, The General Conference of Seventh-day Adventists, 12501 Old Columbia Pike, Silver Spring, Maryland 20904, copyright 1994, pg. 161.

Snyder, Neil H., "His Name is Yahweh," 100 Paradise Circle, Townville, SC. 29689 copyright 2011.

Springfield, M. "Jesus the Almighty". Portland: Parry Mail Advertising Service, copyright 1972.

Stott, John R. W., "Basic Christianity," Wm. B. Eerdmans Publishing Co., 255 Jefferson Ave. S. E. Grand Rapids, Michigan 49503, page 21, copyright Inter-varsity Press, London, 1958, 1971.

The Qur'an, Translated by Abdullah Yusuf Ali, Tahrike Tarsile Qur'an, Inc., Publisher and Distributors of the Holy Qur'an, P.O. Box 731115, Elmhurst, New York 11373-0115, Fifth U.S. Edition, 2000.

Vance, Laura L. "Seventh-day Adventism in Crisis," Gender and Sectarian Change in an Emerging Religion," publication of this work supported by a grant from the Georgia Southwestern State University Foundation, copyright 1999 by the Board of Trustees of the University of Illinois.

Walker, Peter, "The Jesus Way" the Essential Christian Starter Kit," copyright 2009, Monarch Books Wilkinson House Jordan Hill Road, Oxford OX2 8DR.

Walls, Muncia L. "That I May Know Him," Light Ministries P.O. Box 190, Medora, IN 47260, copyright 1993.

About the Author

Will Daniels is a graduate of Youngstown State University, a Vietnam veteran, and a retired industrial engineer. He spends his time reading, writing, and working his Morinda Bioactive business as an independent product consultant. Mr. Daniels is married to his childhood sweetheart, Dorothy. They have three grown children and five grandchildren.